Te

Qualities

A Simple Guide to Well-Being
With 100 Inspiring Affirmations

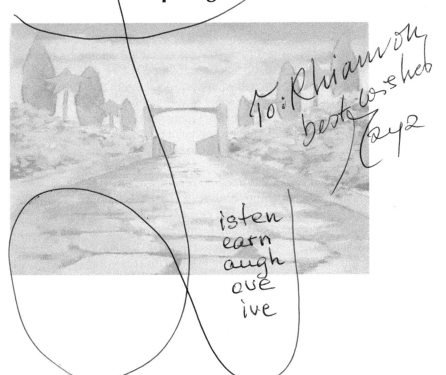

To: Rhiannon
best wishes
Caya

isten
earn
augh
ove
ive

Ten Qualities

ISBN 978-1-849-14277-9

First edition 2012
First published in Great Britain 2012

Copyright Maya Kraus 2012

Yogi Bear photos provided with kind permission of Meta Penca
Front cover design by Clare Hackney
Proof reading by Ruth Rayment

Book production and author mentoring by Tom Evans
The Bookwright
www.thebookwright.com

*For my husband Frank
who was my best friend
and for everyone who misses him*

Also from Maya Kraus

The Journey of a Healer: Main Road and Side Roads

Contents

Part 2: Your Self-help Tools

FOREWORD

I count myself fortunate to be one of the many people who know Maya Kraus. Having recently edited her autobiography, it is clear that she has a fundamental and life-changing effect on all those she meets and touches.

Indeed, an account of my first meeting with Maya is included in this book. As an author myself who weaves open hypnotic loops into his own writing, I will leave it to the reader to work out which case study refers to me.

By the way, in case you don't know what the opening of a hypnotic loop is, you've just read an example of one. I would never have found this out if it weren't for Maya sending me on a new pathway in my life! Just one of the many things I have to be thankful for.

There is a misconception, and even a malaise, in modern society that our health service, with all its wonderful nurses and doctors, are there for us should we get ill. If we have an ache or a pain, we can get a pill for it. If that pill generates side effects, you can even get another pill for that too!

So with all our wonderful technology, we can run our lives as we wish and someone will be there to pick up the pieces should dis-ease visit our door.

Well let me disavow you of that notion should you be harbouring it. There is only one person in the world responsible for your well-being and that is you.

Fortunately, we have a number of miraculous natural healers walking amongst us. They can heal by touch and by thought alone. What's more, the techniques they use can be taught and used by every single human being.

You don't have to be born a healer, you can become one. I know this from first-hand experience and Maya was the catalyst who started switching this 'different-ability' on in me.

All healing too starts with self-healing. If a plane depressurises, they tell you to sort your own oxygen out first so you can better help others. This applies to the healing of our body, mind and spirit.

If you are intrigued by this process and learning to self-heal so you can help yourself and others, this book is a fabulous place to start.

Nothing in this book is complicated. It is all completely safe. It's also free.

Eternal thanks, Maya, for all the healing you have brought to the planet so far and for all the new healers you will enable from reading this book.

Both this book and you are a gift from the heavens.

Tom Evans, Surrey Hills
Author of Flavours of Thought and
Architect of Recipes for Fresh Thinking

PART 1
THE TEN
QUALITIES

INTRODUCTION

The Ten Qualities is the distillation of many years of my practice as a healer. I don't quite know where they came from or why there are ten of them. Perhaps it is because we have ten fingers or that the universe is built from the ten numbers from 0 to 9.

What I now know is that they seem to be universally applicable and they possess the power to heal at a fundamental level.

It is widely agreed that stress and emotional turmoil are the seeds of the vast majority of dis-ease.

This book is a simple-to-apply antidote to anyone so afflicted. I have found that at least 90% of patients I have treated over many years needed help and treatment in this area.

Although my clients often first present themselves as having a health problem, in many cases the root cause is an emotional trauma, very often deeply hidden in childhood experience.

Such problems may manifest themselves in a lack of confidence, low self-esteem and a general lack of direction in life.

Dealing with these problems is complex and may involve specialist help. In my experience, however, I find that application of the Ten Qualities is a great place to start.

Its brilliance is in its simplicity and universal applicability.

It delivers a positive approach to facing difficulties leading rapidly to happy outcomes and improved health.

What is also so amazing about the Ten Qualities is that we can all learn to use them.

UNDERSTANDING STRESS

Good stress is what I call 'creative stress' where the element of challenge brings about a feeling of accomplishment and is therefore positive and rewarding. The key feature here is that the stress is controlled by the individual and not the other way around. Interestingly, the absence of good stress can often bring about problems such as might be experienced by giving up work through retirement or redundancy, or by parents who find that their children have become independent.

Bad stress, in simple terms, is the opposite of good stress. In this situation the stress is corrosive and damaging to health. The causes of negative stress can be many and varied and individual. It is not an easy problem to deal with and strategies to help can take many forms.

Short-term stress is an anxiety that punctuates our lives from time to time, but which is usually resolved satisfactorily, although not always without worrying symptoms. Examples which serve to illustrate the point might include anxiety about an impending interview or an important speech or organising a challenging dinner party.

How Dis-ease can Lead to Disease

Many of us in the modern world live only in our heads and have completely lost touch with awareness and respect for our bodies. We are continually driven to gain social standing, success and prosperity. We block out our body's cries for help. We are driven to keep up appearances.

We try to be physically more attractive by constantly dieting, overtraining, using artificial stimulants to increase energy, taking drugs to combat depression or reaching for painkilling drugs to keep going. These are all just quick fixes. We become so busy with fast living that we lose touch with our body's own wisdom and its energies and so override the body's endurance. Even more damaging, we suppress our feelings and tensions and show the 'stiff upper lip'.

Gradually, we completely lose touch with our most precious friend, our own body.

We forget that our feelings and emotions are known throughout our bodies. Even when the body sends out warning signals in the form of a tight throat, dizziness, nausea or a painful shoulder or knee, we then quickly reach out for drugs.

Dis-ease becomes disease when we don't know how to handle fear, anger, irritation or other emotional states. The communication of our body, mystery and perplexity of its body/brain connection is shut down. We now enter the third degree of stress – we fall ill with disease (often related to inherited weaknesses like arthritis, nervous disorders or asthma) or we experience an injury. I often see a patient for the first time when they have reached this state and they expect a 'quick fix' there and then with regard to their symptoms and ill health.

4

Within these pages, I hope to raise your awareness of your own body, helping you to control stress and to manage what is going on in your life at present. I hope to throw a life-line to you whenever you find yourself stuck in your way forward by awakening a deeper understanding as to who you are, where you come from and where you are now at this moment of life.

I found that by introducing my patients to mastering the 'Ten Qualities' I have helped them to tap into their inner knowledge, and so to move on from a false perception of the outside world to internal trust, vision, calm and peace. When we can move beyond our limited basic beliefs and preconceptions, we can enjoy the challenge of a shifting and rebirthing of our inner self and the energy fields we are surrounded by.

Nutrition and healthy lifestyle are also important aspects for a balanced healthy life. Many wonderful books have been written on these subjects and I have added some titles in Suggested Readings.

It is also important to consider our triad of health: our physical, emotional, nutritional and spiritual needs must all be taken into account. We cannot treat one part of this triad, or triangle, in isolation.

If you can change your mind, you can change your life.

I wish you good health and joy in your new awakened life!

THE TRIAD OF HEALTH

In kinesiology and Touch for Health, the principle for holistic healing is the Triad of Health. The word holistic conveys the idea that 'the whole is greater than just the sum of its parts'. In the context of natural medicine it means considering the whole person; their harmony.

The concept of 'wholism' draws its influence from the Far East. Chinese traditional medicine looks at the whole person, not the symptoms. They believe in vital life force – energy – Qi (or chi) which runs through all the meridians, and which have real physical meanings now.

As we become more and more familiar with energy medicine, we discover that our health is truly holistic and that we are well only if our body and mind cooperate.

We do not treat disease, we treat the whole person. We cannot simply take out one side of the triangle to treat without looking at all three sides.

For perfect health, we have to be like an equilateral triangle – perfectly balanced and poised. A weakness on one side will affect the others and all sides interact and interdepend on each other.

At the centre is our core and our spirit.

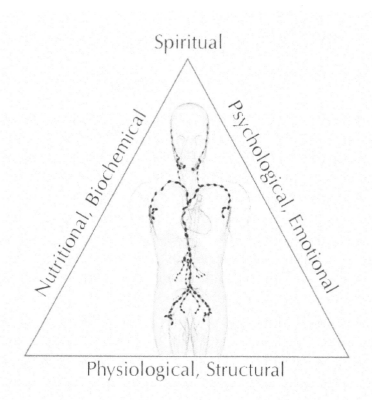

Spiritual

Nutritional, Biochemical

Psychological, Emotional

Physiological, Structural

CHILDHOOD PATTERNING

I would like to help you to understand the complexity of the mind, how childhood patterning can affect the way we act and behave, and how all our emotions are known through our body.

In my work I have found also, on many occasions, a link between mothers who suffered anxiety or severe stress during pregnancy which affected the development of the emotional well-being in the unborn child.

I would like to refer to an article published by the University of Bristol in The Observer by the health editor Jo Revill in 2004. It was entitled 'Mothers' anxiety levels linked to autism and dyslexia' and it researched the lives of over 7000 mothers and children.

Professor Vivette Glover from the Imperial College, London analysed the resulting data and, after examining the level of anxiety and antenatal stress of mothers at 18 weeks of pregnancy, she found that the mother's mood can increase the likelihood of children exhibiting emotional or behavioural problems in their early childhood years. She stressed that, "These findings are only risk factors, not certainties."

I could write a book filled with case histories where my patients displayed a similar level of stress in later life based on the mother's inability to resolve severe tensions or traumas during pregnancy.

Although these inherited traits may not be natural to the character of the child, I call this: 'an inherited emotional DNA.'

An 'Inherited Emotional DNA'

As the child grows up, it will relate subconsciously in its behaviour and actions to those feelings or fears the mother (or even grandmother!) experienced during their pregnancy, even if the circumstances the child or adult might find themselves in, later on in life, are different to those of the mother's. Once these same emotions are triggered, and if not recognised and dealt with, they can stay programmed throughout that person's adult life and, furthermore, other negative attitudes, fears and stressors may develop on top of these – emotions have antennae!

Whenever such an issue has arisen in my work and my patients question their mothers after treatment, they would in almost all cases admit to having suffered a similar emotional state during pregnancy or during their childhood years.

A young mother came to see me suffering increasingly from panic attacks and severe palpitations. She could no longer use the lift to her office, situated on the fifth floor, and her husband had to drive her to work. All the tests and scans from the hospital came back normal. I used health kinesiology and found that she had an issue going back to when she was a three month old foetus in her mother's womb. We released 'a fear of disaster'. Afterwards she contacted her mother who told her that, when she was three months pregnant with her, she had contracted measles.

From then on her mother had suffered from continuous anguish and worries that her child may be born blind.

The development stages of the unborn child

Week 4 to 5 – development of the brain and visibility of cranial nerves, regular heartbeat.

Weeks 5 to 8 – development of primitive reflex actions.

Week 9 – all essential organs have begun to form.

Week 16 – development of vision; babies have been shown to turn their heads when a bright light was pointed at the abdomen of the mother. Baby makes active movements.

Weeks 19 to 21– hearing develops. I heard on the radio that if you play the music of Vivaldi or Mozart, the baby can relate to it after it is born and it could have a calming and reassuring influence when it feels stressed or upset. I recommended this to my daughter-in-law. After Stella was born and whenever she was crying hard, she put on the same CD – it helped little baby Stella to calm down; she would listen intently and fall asleep.

Week 22 – development of muscles and the body becomes more active; mother can feel movements.

Weeks 27 to 30 – rapid brain development, nervous system develops enough to control some bodily functions.

Week 32 – dream state cerebral cortex matures: thinking, feeling, remembering.

In my work I found, when muscle testing, that the unborn child can already perceive emotional patterning from the mother when she is 10 weeks pregnant. Once born, the emotional die is cast (see under 'an inherited emotional DNA'.

In so many cases, the root causes of issues we face in adulthood are seeded at these formative times.

11

The development stages from birth to 18 years old

Birth to 6 months – time to be.

6-18 months – time to do (learning new skills).

18-36 months – time to think for itself.

3-6 years – creating an identity.

6-12 years – developing skills

13-18 years – regenerating (responsibility to the self, reflecting the earlier stages).

Various short-term stressors that the mother experiences during pregnancy may not influence the emotional programming of the unborn child and they don't seem to be damaging.

However, when the stress hormone ACTH (adrenocorticotropic hormone) increases during continual stressful or traumatic experiences of the mother during pregnancy, this could have a direct effect on the unborn child. The child may become anxious or fearful. It might even affect the ease of understanding others or the ease of learning.

Mental or emotional tension with the father, or a close family member, can also place a stamp on the emotional development of the child. It can shape its attitude and aptitude to stress during future years. The support of the father during pregnancy or a close relative or friend can help for the emotional well-being of the mother during pregnancy. The bonding of a partner with the unborn and born child cannot be emphasised enough.

Much research is still ongoing on this complex 'subconscious emotional landscape' and its relationship to the body.

THE TEN QUALITIES AND HOW THEY CAN HELP YOU TO FULFIL YOUR POTENTIAL

Even after treatments like counselling, psychotherapy, kinesiology or hypnotherapy, I have discovered that most of my patients can benefit from further self-work by using the Ten Qualities.

We are all endowed with qualities and talents and it is our birthright to bring these to fruition. I hope to help you understand how childhood conditioning can sometimes hinder one's progress and how to gain freedom in whatever you would like to achieve.

With this book, I would like to guide readers towards a deeper understanding of themselves: why we do the things we do, where we come from (childhood conditioning, or even having an inherited and emotional DNA) and where we are now in this stage of our lives.

As you go through the Ten Qualities' sections you will gain a safe platform on which to build. Discover yourself and allow your conscious brain to experience freedom.

It needs only some mental agility and discipline – intent is energy.

The experiences of life are continually evaluated and processed in our mind. To overcome blocks we need to acknowledge first our past errors or blunders, misconceptions or misunderstandings – they are only lessons to draw from. Remember: whatever happened in your past, you always did your best with the knowledge you had then. You need to accept this, and forgive yourself and others before you can move on. Then tap into a source of talent you never dreamt you had that allows you to discover and embrace a wonderful new world.

Whether or not you are presently feeling despair or undergoing stress management, you will find that the Ten Qualities, when properly understood, can be very helpful in freeing you to change and grow on your journey towards happiness and wholeness. In short they are a helpful aid to overcoming deep insecurities, repressions and stagnation.

HOW BEST TO USE THE TEN QUALITIES

Why not equip yourself with a little exercise book, preferably with a pleasing cover of your choice?

Find a quiet place in your home and reflect on where you are at this stage of your life. Make two columns on the page. List all the positive things and your achievements in the left column and all the negative things and unpleasant obligations in the right one. Then try and figure out what you are missing in your life and what you could achieve.

Allow yourself the indulgence of a little daydreaming and let your inner child play with your imagination and visualise your desires in order to bring them into reality. Never lose hope. Yet try not to let your hope lead you to exaggerated expectations. There is a fine line between hope and unrealistic hope.

When you are clear what you would like most to change in your life, give yourself some loving thoughts – the first step to starting the process for change!

It may be learning an instrument, learning how to dance the salsa, spending more quality time with your family, studying something new or even owning a little house by the sea.

Remember you have the power to live your dreams.

Once you have set a clear goal, you are ready to begin your journey. This will energise your life and invigorate your will. The moment you decide to become a changed person – the real you – your mind no longer has its limitations. Your consciousness extends in all directions and you can raise your life to higher levels. A new and wonderful world opens up and allows you to discover dormant talents.

Meanwhile, try and clear unwanted clutter in your home. Your home reflects your mind!

There are many helpful books. You may learn from the experiences of others who have handled the challenges that you yourself may be currently facing in one form or another. There are many autobiographies available about great people who succeeded in moving beyond their limitations. Take note and learn their approaches for success.

Stop making excuses – you need willpower to help you to succeed. Any cynicism or doubt can endanger success.

Be energetic and inspired by your vision!

Be positive! Only then can you achieve your goal. Keep your goal simple and don't overcomplicate your changes. You may need to give in order to receive. Start by giving yourself time and self-love.

Gratitude to others is an important key when you make changes. Acknowledge your successes and all that is good in your world and even your failures. Only then can you move forward.

Now we are going to consider some practical approaches for achieving your goals.

If you are uncertain as to which quality section is the one to work on, you could visit a kinesiologist who can muscle test you. Or, why not invite a friend to work with you on the muscle testing techniques, listed under Muscle Testing.

Once you are confident with the techniques, go through the list of all the qualities pages. Say each quality section aloud and then muscle test, one quality at a time. It might surprise you that your body will indicate, via your subconscious, a completely different quality to the one that you thought you needed.

You might feel tempted to start with the quality we seek most – freedom. However, only once you have understood and taken on the first nine qualities, are you ready to learn about 'understanding freedom'.

If we want to heal our fellow beings and the Earth, we need to heal ourselves first.

HOW I FOUND THE AFFIRMATIONS FOR SELF-EMPOWERMENT

When one of my patients came back for treatment, muscle testing indicated that he needed an affirmation. I was most surprised to find that the very same mantra I gave him previously still needed to be dealt with. He assured me that he was reading the affirmation many times every day.

My intuition led me to apply the ACMOS method devised by Dr René Naccachian, Paris, and with whom I had had the privilege of studying. ACMOS is short for Analysis of the Compatibility of Matter on the Organism and its Synergy. It is in essence a biofeedback energy tester.

When in China, Dr Naccachian suffered from a very painful knee. In desperation, he reluctantly accepted a treatment in acupuncture. Within one day he managed to walk again without pain. This led him to a desire to scientifically understand what had occurred during his treatment of acupuncture. He spent over thirty years of research and his study led to qualifications in the fields of biophysics and bioenergetics. He also qualified as a doctor in science and energetic medicine and holds a PhD in molecular biology.

His research led him to invent the ACMOS biofeedback energy-testing system that I could use to scientifically verify my theories of how affirmations work when spoken out loud.

So I applied the ACMOS instrument on my patient's acupuncture points, taking note of the readings. Then I asked my patient to repeat the affirmations silently. There was no change in the reading. Then he read the affirmations out loud three times and, to our surprise, the energy reading moved up by a number of points. This led me to believe that whatever we read silently, although it may be informative and attractive to our minds, it does not tonify the energy of our bodies.

This proves that we need to say affirmations aloud for them to be effective. The above test, which I now have repeated on numerous occasions, demonstrates that we can energise our bodily system and activate positive thinking when we say affirmations out loud. I recommend saying the affirmations every morning on waking and before going to bed, and whenever you have a quiet moment to yourself.

Try also to look into your eyes in a mirror when you say these. Repeat them a number of times. After one or two weeks you will embrace the meaning of the affirmations and you will find that you remember them without looking at your notes! This is when they will help you to change your mental point of view and so become part of you and your ways.

THE TEN QUALITIES

1. ENJOYMENT

"Just trust yourself, then you will know how to live."

Johann Wolfgang von Goethe (1749-1832)

When I was little, I remember my mother saying to me when she kissed me goodnight: "Tomorrow is another happy day." This always puzzled me, especially when I had a 'bad' day: falling over and cutting my knee open, or a little friend telling me that she didn't want to play with me anymore. However, the thought of having a happy day made me feel instantly comforted and I started to make new plans for the next day.

Many of us go about our days unengaged and empty; we are simply not enjoying ourselves.

When you get up in the morning, say, "Today, I'll take things light and easy."

You will see how your mind becomes instantly peaceful.

When you approach life with equanimity, you are open to learning more. Enjoyment comes when you open yourself to your feelings and this in turn makes it easy to return them. In order to give you the need to be involved, once you have opened yourself to the world, your newly kindled interest in the world can trigger your energy and enthusiasm for a fascinating new life and new experiences.

We don't always have the choice of a perfect work environment and we cannot change the personalities of our colleagues, or family members whom we are living with to suit ourselves. It comes down to your attitude and your inner knowledge of yourself not to be put off by them. We have many preconceptions about the people around us which might make us want to fit in with them and accept them. Once you let go of these opinions – often built upon other people's opinions – you can fit in with all kinds of personalities and not be put off by them. And you will discover that your positive thoughts create enjoyment for you and others.

Be peaceful within yourself and open to experience. A closed mind will miss out on new opportunities and lead us to a negative place.

To attract enjoyment and involvement you need good energy to incite your desires. There is no use sitting behind a closed door and waiting for someone to open it for you. You could be waiting forever. You are the only one who can let go of this unproductive self-restricting way. The same goes if you are waiting for someone to change your life. There is no need to carry a suit of armour; remember you can always change your actions and your responses. By simply changing a negative thought about someone and smiling at them, the other person gets a signal and you will surprise yourself – they will smile back. If you feel good, so will those around you.

Whenever you pass a mirror, look at yourself and give yourself a big smile. Then apply that smile in the presence of others – you will be amazed how people respond to you.

Can you see how easy it is using these simple steps in this chapter and how the old conditioning just passes away?

I have chosen the following case history to show you how easily you can become disconnected, and therefore unable to enjoy the things you once loved to do.

A 24-year-old lady asked me if I could help her: "I have stress at work, stress at home. I have also suffered a migraine once or twice a week since the age of 16. I was diagnosed with endometriosis when I was 18 years old and my periods are so painful that I often have to take a day off work. I have been suffering from flu symptoms for the past two weeks – and I can't stop crying."

At this point she burst into tears. From her completed patient form, I learned that she was a qualified silversmith. Also, she had only recently been discharged from hospital having been treated for a pulmonary embolism and was on the drug Warfarin and anti-depressants.

Thank God for muscle testing, I would not have known otherwise where to start!

During allergy testing I discovered that she had a gluten allergy and I adjusted her diet. A stress issue was the next priority her body wanted me to deal with. It indicated that she felt trapped in her life and constantly put-upon.

After stress release using health kinesiology, she suddenly came to realise that, even as a small child, she had tried very hard to get her father's attention. He was always stern with her. When she was nine years old, he bought her a pair of red shoes. He smiled at her and told her that she was very pretty wearing red shoes and a ponytail. This was the first time she remembered him smiling at her.

"I am still wearing red shoes," she added apologetically, "and I hate my hair."

I looked down at her feet and, indeed, she was wearing red suede trainers and also wore her hair up in a ponytail.

I gave her some breathing exercises and an affirmation to say aloud, many times a day:

> *"I can do what I think is right. I can do what I need to do. I am important. I am creative and I love myself."*

Three months after her fifth treatment she returned. She told me that she had not suffered from a single migraine since she first came to see me and she had begun making jewellery in her garden shed. Her menstrual cycles had become more regular and she no longer suffered from cramping pains.

"And I bought some new shoes," she added with a huge smile.

I looked down at her feet – her shoes were a beautiful blue!

Enjoy every second; the hours will follow by themselves.

VERIFICATIONS AND AFFIRMATIONS

"I will now give myself a holiday from my past and the old self-defeatism. I believe now in my inner strength and talents, which will guide me to make positive changes in my life and I am ready to open up to new opportunities."

"I will move beyond my limitations and am willing to take action. I am open to change and to getting involved."

"I am enthusiastic in what I do and I do not need to please someone else."

"I now turn my back on old attitudes and inhibiting beliefs. I accept responsibility for my own life."

"It is my birthright to enjoy myself."

"I believe in myself."

"I now embrace the abundance of good things so they will invigorate and improve my life."

"I now recognise the richness of my meaningful thoughts and I realise my dreams."

"'I trust in the innate wisdom of the universe."

"I am already a success."

"I am FREE to be ME!"

2. GIVING, GRATITUDE AND HUMILITY

"God, give us grace to accept with serenity the things that cannot be changed, courage to change the things which should be changed, and the wisdom to distinguish the one from the other."

Reinhold Niebuhr, The Serenity of Prayer (1934)

Giving has its roots in having insight and generosity towards the future by giving what you can in the now.

There must be balance of give and take in giving.

In your well-meant effort to help others and in your readiness to help, do not 'trouble the waters' by being overly helpful – you cannot rescue everyone. In a work situation this can cause you to 'overwork' and lead to ill health. Learn to say no when you feel it is appropriate. People will respect you for it.

You need to be open and have respect towards the knowledge of others. Accept that every person has gifts of certain talents in one way or another. Keep a healthy attitude – you can learn from others.

Very often we function from a false conception of safeguarding ourselves. When you let go, life becomes easier and easier. Have faith in yourself, be positive and let go of all your doubts that don't serve you any longer. Then you can be helpful in your giving.

We do not need to possess control to interfere with other people's situations. If someone is in need of help, first listen. Then use your logic and wisdom. You can say only what has helped you in the past, and simply suggest what you feel is helpful or whatever is needed to lighten someone's distress. Then leave it up to the individual to make their own decisions.

Before we can be useful to others, we need to look at ourselves. We all have a store of power of wisdom and compassion. Always use it wisely and keep active at it.

When you help others and show your compassion you will in due time find that those others will in turn accept you more readily. It is a two-way process. Do unto others as you would have done unto yourself.

Sometimes we hold back from giving. You need to learn to trust others and this starts with trusting yourself. If you hold back you may be nursing a deep-rooted suspicion of hurt or disappointment. See yourself without old grievances that are no use to you. This is how we can grow and have giving in balance.

In order to give we need to learn to give to ourselves first. When you constantly give out and your 'reservoir of giving' to yourself is empty, look at yourself and give yourself love and forgiveness. Are we relaxed and at ease with ourselves? Very often, when we give advice, we need to distinguish between clear and confused thoughts.

To learn giving you need to learn to be balanced within yourself and always keep your options open.

You will find that, by safely reaching out, it will eventually find its way back to you in one form or other. We don't give to be liked. When giving, give from your heart and don't expect gratitude, then you won't feel hurt. Hurt can easily lead to disappointment, resentment and bitterness. Be grateful for the little things that come your way.

Giving is an inner journey; leave your baggage behind. Without love and compassion we cannot heal ourselves and others.

Humility is to accept your own free will and to be open for the willingness to move into action. Then you can be considerate and thoughtful of your own or other people's needs.

It pays great dividends to show humility in social interactions. This requires you to possess inner knowledge of who you really are. Only then can you be comfortable with others, be it with friends, family or at work. To be humble is when you step away from irrational expectations, when you are aware that solutions can't be forced.

Allow some fresh breeze, needed for seeing the 'big picture' free of distractions, to enter your mind. And know that you do not have to be a servant without your wishes.

Humility is not blaming others or yourself for your actions – the latter is self-reproach. Whenever you are using only your own concern you can pass on discomfort. By using rational generosity we have the ability to act responsibly and we can take care of our own or someone else's needs. Whatever happened to upset you during your or another person's life's episodes, remember that any actions taken at that time were done with the best knowledge that you or that other person had.

We all need help sometimes. Don't be proud and use courage to ask.

Greed, selfishness and egotism are the opposite of giving. When we give unconditionally, we bring JOY to others and to ourselves!

A patient of mine brought me her 74-year-old mother to see if I could help her to deal with her depression. Upon sitting, the dear little lady crossed her legs, clasped her hands and slumped forward so intensely that I was unable to view her eyes.

I began to use Touch for Health to tonify her muscles to help her body to straighten up a little. Muscle testing also indicated an issue to be dealt with. Her priority item was a fear of giving.

After the treatment she told me that her husband was very demanding and controlling to such an extent that he would not allow her to help herself to more potatoes (or other foods) than he had on his plate. She came back for a follow-up treatment.

This time I could see her eyes – they were an amazing violet blue!

Two days later she phoned me in distress: "I think I have done a terrible thing. I fancied an extra helping of potatoes. As I placed them on my plate, my husband shot me a threatening look. I finished my food, then got up and slammed the door behind me. On the one hand I felt really good about my boldness, but at the same time I was worried what my husband was going to do. Cautiously, I peered through the door and saw my husband's shocked expression with his mouth wide open. Do you think I went too far?"

I told her that I was proud of her and to come back for another treatment to help her with her self-confidence and how to be comfortable when making her own choices.

Remember: giving and humility last!

VERIFICATIONS AND AFFIRMATIONS

"I now give myself a break and let go of all hurt and I forgive others and myself."

"I can truly forgive and love myself."

"I believe in myself and I attract only loving relationships." "I am generous and I make my own choices."

"I have confidence and trust in myself. It is safe to give and receive nurturing without past constraints."

"I now put all judgements and blame of others and of myself aside."

"I can give to those who ask as best as I can."

"I now forgive those who have been disloyal and manipulative towards me."

"It is safe for me to give freely without the need to give away my competency and without fear of abandonment or rejection."

"I am courageous and can give and receive in equal measures."

"I am FREE to be ME!"

3. CREATIVITY AND FULFILMENT

"Every moment of your life is infinitely creative and the universe is endlessly bountiful. Just put forth a clear enough request and everything your heart desires must come to you."

Shakti Gawain, Creative Visualisation

We all have deep-seated longings for fulfilment. To understand the meaning of fulfilment we need to focus on all those unlived feelings, dreams and emotions we had during our childhood.

I was once told the following story: in an infant school, children were asked to raise their hands if they thought they were an artist. All but one put up their hands. The one who abstained was actually very gifted at drawing. I remembered this when, one day, during my time teaching the violin at schools, the music director sent me ten children for me to check whether I felt they were talented enough to learn to play a string instrument.

I tested these children to see if they could sing in tune and had a good feel for rhythm – all the ingredients needed to study a string instrument. They all passed the test. Then I remembered the above question of the nursery teacher and I was most curious to try this test myself.

I asked: "Who among you thinks they can become a great violinist?"

Everybody's hands shot up with eager anticipation, except for two boys. When I asked one of them why he was not interested, he replied: "I want to be a drummer boy."

The other little chap of seven years old, whom I will refer to as Tommy, told me: "I am rubbish."

When I asked him: "Who told you so?" he replied: "My big brother."

I was very surprised since, during my tests, I noticed that he had a beautiful voice and his tuning was excellent.

I got in touch with his mother and we formed a team whereby the mother came to my lessons to help and encourage Tommy to practise hard at home. As a result, he passed all his violin exams with distinction. Later on I learned that he was accepted to continue his music studies at the Royal Academy of Music in London and I was invited to come to his debut concert at the Wigmore Hall.

In those days children were encouraged by the local councils to learn instruments. Music tuition was given by peripatetic teachers (music teachers who travelled between schools) and some instruments were even supplied to pupils free of charge. Surrey County Council, whom I worked for at that time, sponsored gifted children and the Surrey Council Youth Orchestra was founded.

The orchestra enjoyed giving many concerts in prestigious concert halls, such as the Guildford Civic Hall (now G Live), the London Festival Hall and the Royal Albert Hall.

My language knowledge proved useful also in the organisation of concert tours abroad, in collaboration with the parents' committee. We always travelled with one of the national winners of the BBC Young Musician of the Year to perform concerts with us, both at home and abroad in France and Germany.

The standard was outstanding and some of these young soloists have since become distinguished names in the musical world, such as Lucy Parham and Emma Johnson.

Sadly, free music tuition was axed some years ago and who knows what talents have been locked away forever by lost opportunities.

It is unfortunate when young people don't have the opportunity, support and stimulation to be creative. As demonstrated in the story above, it only needs one small, careless comment (in this case, it was a jealous brother) and the damage is done. I found that creativity is very often taken out of our children from an early age. We have to obey rules because of preconditioning.

Everyone has creativity in themselves, some more than others. Not everyone is born to be a famous artist, pianist, sports personality or garden designer. Sadly, there are so many gifted children who have never been encouraged and who have such low self-esteem that they remain unfulfilled. We need to understand to draw the line and get down to basics. Art is important – a form of problem solving. It helps us to think in a non-linear way. The end result teaches us to think and to create a little time for ourselves to do the things we like best, even if our finished artwork does not end up hanging on the wall.

Whenever we feel overtaken and stuck in our work environment or bored with our daily routine – or lack of routine – art can become a wonderful outlet or first aid to turn our inhibition into a positive form. There is some value in this when we put those constraints into action. There is nobody standing behind you to watch every move and you are not being judged. You are in control of your time to do just this: what you enjoy the most!

I experienced how someone made good use of a situation and turned it into a little indulgence for himself; however odd it seemed at the time.

On our flight back from Toronto, my husband and I found ourselves seated in the middle of a six-seater row, with only one seat left unoccupied next to me. With great relief we quickly placed our newspapers and small bags on the free seat.

Just before take-off we noticed a man of considerable girth appear and make his way down the aisle. We both held our breath. What we feared became a reality. He stopped in front of us and claimed the empty seat, immediately taking over not one but both armrests. He then took off his shoes. This was not all.

To our amazement he produced some embroidery from his travel bag and began working on a half-finished picture showing a little Tyrolean house, surrounded by mountains. We watched him how he skillfully started to fill in pink geraniums trailing from wooden window boxes. It took us both some time to recover from suppressing our laughter. However, I silently saluted his family who might have been the source of encouragement to support their son to enjoy what he was doing, regardless of the circumstances.

Whether you find yourself on the creative or the recipient side of an artistic experience, the reward is the same: enjoyment !

Whenever someone came up to me after a concert to express their appreciation, very often they apologetically added: "Unfortunately I am not a musician." I would answer: "Without music lovers like you we would not have been able to perform in this beautiful hall."

Artists need people to appreciate what they do and have learned – it is part of their reward. Likewise, by giving or receiving enjoyment we allow diversity into our lives and experience fulfilment on every level. Now, ask yourself: 'What has happened to my creative spark?'

"Every child is an artist." – Pablo Picasso

VERIFICATIONS AND AFFIRMATIONS

"I take things light and easy."

"I am able to pursue the plans of my own choice and can take my skills further."

"It is safe for me to show my very own potential."

"I do not always need to wait for permission to do what I want."

"I release all my parental conditioning from the past which blocks my creativity."

"I use my creativity in positive ways."

"I give myself permission to allow enjoyment and creativity to come through."

"I now release stagnation and allow in change and abundance at every level."

"'I open myself up to my willingness to be creative and fulfilled."

"I deserve to be creative and fulfilled."

"I am FREE to be ME!"

4. RESPONSIBILITY AND CONSIDERATION

"Being born as humans to this earth is a very sacred trust.

"We have a sacred responsibility because of the special gift we have, which is beyond the fine gifts of the plant life, the fish, the woodlands, the birds, and all the other living things on Earth. We are able to take care of them."

Audrey Shenandoah, Care for the Land, from the Haudenosaunee Address to the Western World, (1977)

Respect and honour are key for this quality.

We are all responsible for our own actions. What we send out will come back in one form or other. So take care of your thoughts and pause before you speak. Your thoughts can become like a powerhouse of untamed messages, which can prevent you from thinking clearly and being responsible for your actions. You need to be willing to open your mind and see the whole picture.

Through adopting responsibility for our thoughts and actions we also liberate ourselves.

When you have negative beliefs, take note and stop making excuses. Learn from your actions and move on. Then focus on your strengths and trust in your intuition.

Remember: your life is your pursuit and whenever things are not going according to your expectations, do not blame others. You may have invited it, so respond with dignity.

Sometimes you may find yourself obliged to do something against your wishes.

Simply shift your attitude. Don't be content with things as they are. You can make the difference and enjoy doing it too.

Ask yourself these questions:

- "Do I enjoy doing the work that earns me a living?"
- "Am I happy and fulfilled with my work?"
- "Do I feel that I am merely 'existing'?"
- "Do I leave responsibility to others?"
- "Do I repeatedly do what I do not want to do?"
- "Is my only endeavour in life to make a living and only strive for financial rewards?"

It may not be practical to make immediate changes. However, this should not stop you from planning ahead. Consider your priorities. Domestic or professional demands may have to be answered first.

Whenever you find yourself in a difficult situation, stay alert and make plans to achieve your potential, bearing in mind the need to regard other people's concerns and taking into account their own circumstances.

A thirty-one-year-old lady came to see me shortly after having been hospitalised. She was suffering from ulcerated colitis, loss of weight and had not menstruated for two years. These health problems started very soon after her honeymoon in Bali. During her honeymoon, she and her husband had survived the bombing at a nightclub on Kuta Beach. Although they escaped this horrendous ordeal with only minor injuries, it was nevertheless a very traumatic experience for them.

I started the treatment by releasing the trauma and then adjusted her diet to allow her body to become more acid-/alkaline-balanced.

She also needed some digestive enzymes and goldenseal (a wonderful healing herb to soothe her colitis).

At our next session I invited her to take a closer look at the responsibility and consideration qualities.

"Yes," she suddenly realised, "Recently, I am easily offended and angry when I feel overlooked. I have become increasingly selfish, constantly mentally irritated and impatient with everybody and my surroundings. I feel numb and indifferent, even towards my husband. Since Bali I have not taken responsibility in my marriage for fear that something unexpected will destroy our happiness."

She needed a number of further treatments, and three months after her initial visit she told me that she had learned to be more cooperative and reliable to herself. "I am no longer afraid of the future and I have become more involved with the people around me. My menstrual cycle restarted two weeks ago, and my consultant was impressed to find that my digestive problem had improved so much so that he did not see the need for me to come back. Even my relationship with my husband has become happy again!"

It is your birthright to enjoy life. Taking responsibility for yourself and having consideration for others will make this happen.

VERIFICATIONS AND AFFIRMATIONS

"I am thoughtful, friendly and kind to myself and others."

"I am accountable for my own actions and decision-making."

"I am conscientious, reliable and trustworthy."

"I am in charge of, and responsible for, my own life."

"I always respond with dignity. I am dependable."

"I am open to new opportunities."

"I am disciplined and considerate on my way to future achievements."

"I trust myself and I do not need to ask others what to do."

"I trust the process of my learning and live in perfect equilibrium and harmony with myself, others and nature."

"I now act responsibly and wisely with all my relationships that are important to me."

"I am FREE to be ME!"

5. CONFIDENCE AND TRUST

"You must begin to trust yourself. If you do not then you will forever be looking to others to prove your merit to you, and you will never be satisfied.

"You will always be asking others what to do and at the same time resenting those from whom you seek such aid."

Jane Roberts, The Nature of Personal Reality

"If only I had the confidence to do what I really, really want, then my dreams could come true."

Does this sound familiar?

To gain confidence in whatever you do, you need to know exactly what it is that you want and how to achieve it.

Firstly you need to ask yourself: why do I do the things I do? What do I need to make some changes?

Once you have a clear vision of this, you can move forward with a plan of action. Consider all the facts and don't be put off by obstacles. Trust your first impression – your footprint, whether coming from an intuitive feeling or an inner vision, and don't let others put you off with their own preferred pros and cons. Just listen to their advice, discern what could be useful and discard what does not fit into your plan.

Then go for it, use the feelings of your first intuition and set forth with your timing. Believing in yourself will give you the needed enthusiasm and confidence to see your project to fruition. Remember that having a goal can already energise your life!

There is nothing wrong with setting material goals. Financial rewards may not necessarily pave your path to fulfilment, but as long as you use them with humility, these goals can still help build your confidence.

You may find that, by working wisely with your intuition and inner messages and, of course, a clear plan, you can move past old conditioning and past emotional scarring – all part of your building blocks – to learn from experience, good or bad. You will be able to grow from these lessons and, once understood, you will have the power and enthusiasm to follow your dreams.

Once you find what you really would like to do, try not to focus too intensively on the end result. The results you are looking for will happen before you know it, as long as you are well focussed and you mean it.

Be comfortable with yourself, your personality and your own creative instincts, as these will help you to empower yourself and enable you to take full responsibility for your own life. Living in the past will only hold you back. Because you were poor as a child, or something happened in the past to block your confidence, do not surrender and think that you will never get anywhere.

Self-defeatism can eat up your self-esteem and self-confidence. Simply stop self-blame and blaming others. Give yourself a break from your unproductive 'mind-talk'. It is up to you and only you to change your responses.

When you value yourself, even your relationships will change and you will attract people who appreciate you. If you are continually looking at others for advice as to what to do, you will never be confident or satisfied.

Not trusting can create suspicion and can lead to despair. From time to time and at the end of the day, ask yourself: "Did I undermine someone?"

You need to have a strong will to shed the chains of having been a prisoner of the past. Do not accuse others and everything for your upbringing or whatever forced you to become a weak human being. Only your own will can help you to move on – it is only waiting for your instructions and is ready for you to go into action for sound decision-making.

Stop making excuses for yourself and apply self-discipline, at first in tiny steps. This will throw you a lifeline to persevere when the going is hard. There is no 'quick fix.

Fear of failure is only a test and it is often self-made. It is important not to be put off when life throws you unforeseen 'bumps' – see them as a challenge and remind yourself what you are passionate about. Never take your eye off your objectives if you want to succeed and grow. See any setbacks as a friend who is challenging you to achieve the goal you have set for yourself.

A charming young man came to see whether kinesiology could help. Since childhood he had suffered from a painful knee, which had prevented him from engaging in sporting activities. Recently he had had various tests and X-rays, but they all came back negative.

"I can't even walk my dog," he said. I asked him whether he could remember when the problem with his knee had started.

"When I was nine years old, I was hit by a car. I was one of seven children and my mother was constantly stressed looking after us. I didn't want to worry her so I didn't tell her."

I checked his muscular system and found that the tibial muscle was weak. The posterior tibia acts as a stabiliser of the ankle, helps to flex the foot out and upwards and can often be in spasm when associated with other weak muscles. This can directly affect other muscles and by way of compensating, can cause a painful knee.

After a muscle-balancing treatment in Touch for Health he hardly noticed any discomfort when moving his leg and he was quite impressed with the result.

I noticed from his patient form that he was taking medication for high blood pressure. When I asked him whether he was happy with his life in general, he told me that he had found a wonderful partner, but that he had got too personally involved with the financial targets he had to deal with in his work. "Maybe I push myself too hard," he explained. "I have been thinking of myself recently, of what I really would like to do," he added.

We addressed the problem he had with his work. I pointed out to him that he needed to understand how, from an early stage in his life, he was expected to be loyal to his family. In order to see things in perspective and to become more confident in recognising his own needs, he had to learn to be loyal to himself also. The homework I gave him to do was to say "no", at least once a day. In order to learn to trust himself to venture out to new opportunities, I gave him the quality section of confidence and trust.

After a number of follow-up treatments he came back to tell me: "My leg is no longer bothering me and I can now walk my dog. I have also set up my own business and am presently writing my first book."

When I took his blood pressure, I was pleased with the result and asked him to see his doctor to adjust his blood pressure tablets.

Trust your mind, trust your heart and continue on your path of creating a definitive purpose in your life. There is no need for boundaries, denial or delusions, nor the need to change other people.

Just stop worrying and trust yourself!

VERIFICATIONS AND AFFIRMATIONS

"It is OK to be independent without guilt."

"It is safe for me to trust my intuition and instincts."

"I now release all fears blocking my goals and I am open for change."

"'I am worthy of change and of finding my own path."

"I allow others to use their intuition."

"I use my confidence wisely and responsibly"'

"I am dependable."

"'I am my own person and allow myself to move on with confidence."

"I feel secure and have trust and confidence in my future."

"I now move on to the road of my own progress and self-discovery with patience and confidence."

"I now release all negative attachments to everyone and everything that doesn't serve me anymore."

"I am FREE to be ME!"

6. DETACHMENT

"Attachment is the great fabricator of illusions;

Reality can be attained only by someone who is detached."

Simone Weil (1909-1943)

If you are not sure of the meaning of detachment, this is for you! Are you holding on to anything or anyone? To learn detachment is about challenging the energies of your ego to stay in balance. It comes down to thinking and allowing yourself to be free to flow with life. To achieve this, you need to liberate yourself from your habit of constantly worrying for others or being controlled by them. When you are worried, your thoughts become like a powerhouse of seeds and, before you know it, you are overtaken by them.

To be of help to others and yourself, you need to recognise your borderlines where detachment starts and where involvement begins. This needs a well-grounded and strong personality in order to weigh up situations and not get constantly caught up in other people's demands and struggles. Look out for the things that are draining your energies and what you suppress, and what it is that tips the scales of your freedom.

When we learn to be comfortable with ourselves, we get closer to creating an insight of learning the positive qualities of detachment. When you override your comfort zone you lose touch with the world around you.

Ask yourself: Do I easily switch off when I feel incompatible with others?

Then create a little personal space in your thinking and stop procrastinating. You have the ability to use your potential to communicate freely. Focus on what is draining you and what you suppress. Then use your positive qualities to boost your enthusiasm and motivation. Remember, you do not need to be controlled by others and it is your negativity that allows others to divert you from your true calling.

At the same time allow others to support you, to a point, and stay strong when you feel that you are being overpowered by your own free will. Closed-mindedness can hold you back in your life's endeavours. When we feel increasingly withdrawn from people and nature around us, we can easily lose contact with the feelings of our own body and we basically just live in our heads.

Know exactly where you are going and what your life's purpose is.

Allow yourself to practise detachment with a live-and-let-live attitude and allow others to be who they are.

Some years ago I met a young artist who sought help with IBS (Irritable Bowel Syndrome). Her posture said it all.

She sat with hunched shoulders and looked very pale. She was dressed in black, right down to her tights. After adjusting her diet, we addressed a number of repressed negative emotions, which seemed to stop her from pursuing her painting career.

When I questioned her about her choice of black clothing, she said, "I always wear black, it's easier."

I suggested to her that she try to wear a bit more colour for the next visit. At her following appointment she was still wearing black clothes but had added a tasteful maroon and beige striped scarf. "As you see, I made an effort, but this is all I could manage on colour for this time," she said apologetically.

After three further treatments of diet and stress release, all her physical symptoms had receded except on each occasion when the telephone rang, she exclaimed, "This made my stomach turn into a knot."

On further questioning she told me how terrified she felt every time she heard the phone in case it was her mother at the other end. Her mother was a very sad person and phoned her almost every day to unload all her unhappiness onto her daughter. She even blamed her for the break-up of her marriage. The poor girl was made to feel guilty every time. I asked her to look at the list of Ten Qualities and to choose one that might help her to continue her painting career. She pointed at creativity.

Muscle testing, however, indicated that the quality of detachment was what she really needed in order to liberate her thoughts and to let go of blame and shame. Only a peaceful mind could rekindle her artistic talents. I gave her the list of the verifications and affirmations of detachment and an additional mantra for self-love, to say aloud a few times every day.

I didn't hear from her again until two years later, when I received an invitation to a private preview of her art exhibition. Enclosed was a thank-you message in which she wrote that she found my treatment, especially the quality of detachment, most helpful in regaining her inspiration, confidence and peace in her work. She also mentioned that the affirmations had improved her relationship with her mother.

When I arrived at the preview, I could hardly recognise her in her most attractive colourful outfit. As I was about to leave, she asked me which of her paintings I liked the most. I pointed at one which caught my eye, but had a 'reserved' notice attached to it. She said that she didn't want to part with this painting, since it was the first work she had undertaken after my treatment. Then she took it off the wall and said to me, "This is yours!"

Remember, you do not need the approval of others. Work on your own consciousness and believe in yourself. When you feel stuck, be it in your relationship at home or at work, try to understand the other person. At the same time understand that, in order to be successful in your endeavours and not become subservient or a doormat, never lose the ability to be in tune with yourself – your own standard. You may not always be successful in your expectations of pleasing someone. Listen and believe in your self-worth, which comes from within you. Stop sitting back when you are being criticised. Acknowledge the criticism or hurtful remarks, learn from them, and then move on.

To learn detachment is about doing something for yourself and this needs your concentrated effort in order to learn how to manage your emotions. This way you can live effectively in all situations. You know you can change, by simply changing your thoughts.

When your energies are challenged, ask yourself:

"Where is the problem?"

Then tell yourself: "It is only in my mind!"

VERIFICATIONS AND AFFIRMATIONS

"I am comfortable with myself and I can use my potential to the full."

"I no longer need to be overpowered by other people's demands."

"I am in tune with my own relationship."

"I believe in my own successes and learn from my own failures. I am bold and I know when it is safe to stick to my own principles."

"It is safe for me to open new doors to become involved in new experiences."

"I have the power within me to achieve what I desire."

"It is safe to be true to my motivations and to myself."

"I can learn and listen to other people's problems without being challenged."

"I can stand my own ground. I know that I can pursue my own true purpose in life."

"I am free to function to do what is best for the universe and me."

"I am FREE to be ME!"

7. FLEXIBILITY AND BALANCE

"A happy gracious flexibility." – *Pericles calls this quality of the Athenians: lucidity of thought, clearness and propriety of language, freedom from prejudice and freedom from stiffness, openness of mind, amiability of manners."*

From *Eutrapelia* by Matthew Arnold, Irish Essays, Speech at Eton (1882)

Life could be such an easy ride if only frustration would not get in the way.

Flexibility means to have the capacity to change with the circumstances.

Tradition and following only your own ways can cause inflexibility and this in turn does not help you to feel good in yourself. We need to be creative to learn this quality and love ourselves to be confident – it can mean that sometimes we need to learn to sacrifice for others. When we feed only on our own personality and rigidity, this can become, in time, destructive. We need to learn to leave our own comfort zone and experience and explore new information and possibilities. We generally use old experiences to create attitudes towards old patterns which then can become ingrained into our existing lifestyle.

One can easily recognise an inflexible person by their rigid physical posture. Do you suffer from a stiff neck or shoulder tension? When your life's energy tank is on overflow and you ignore signals from your body crying enough is enough, you become a prisoner of your own doing which in turn could lead to physical health problems.

Truth can hurt but it can also heal you if you are willing to let go of your old crutches.

Are they truly worth defending? It all sums up to what your world view is, how you fit into it, who you are and where you belong. If you find yourself constantly on the old road you can become deadly boring and more and more inflexible; in fact, very irritated and only existing. This does not serve your gall bladder or liver function well.

The key to good relationships, whether at work or with people around you, is creating a good and agreeable communication as well as trust and, most of all, – practising empathy. We are faced daily with unexpected challenges at work. If you are overly conscientious you may find that you have problems with adjusting. Try to focus on the positive qualities of your work colleagues and don't pay attention to those with negative views. Understand that other people also struggle towards fulfilment in their challenging lives and give them due respect. Recognise that they are vulnerable and they act with the knowledge they have. Life is not about us alone. To be nonjudgmental does not happen until you have made changes within yourself and your inner thoughts. Once recognised, we can easily release tensions.

When faced with a busy schedule ahead, always allow at least half an hour's leeway for unforeseen circumstances.

We are all challenged every day by unexpected confrontations and issues that do not fit into our way of handling problems. Simply go with the flow; let life flow through you and live in the present! Use your willpower to hold your tongue when you disagree with something and be ready to understand that each person's ideas and reactions are different from your own conceptions. Try to be respectful and use diplomacy in your answers. There is always a way to handle unforeseen barriers – see them as a challenge and move on.

The hardest route to conquering inflexibility is not to control others, but to try to understand their opinions and be willing to learn. When we feel discomfort, this simply means that your own body is communicating with you. No matter what the issue is, remember it derives from a thought pattern that can easily be changed.

To learn flexibility we need to learn how to balance our goals – what you want to learn and achieve from them – and not to be overrun by greed. Very careful evaluation as to what is 'good' and what is 'wrong' needs to be assessed and balanced out. Only when you can express yourself without fear of judgement and allow others to be the way they are can you gain respect from others as you show them that you are open to new concepts. At the same time you do not need to be caught up with other people's problems. Try and focus on your own integrity, honesty and positive qualities and be open to other people's inspirations and ideas.

When you are confronted with unexpected troubling emotions, try to apply a more unbiased attitude. As your attitude changes you find that you become more agreeable and are open to other people's points of view. You will find that this can change the atmosphere in which you interact with others and you will have neither a problem, nor difficulty with them and they will have no hardship with you.

Try to eliminate any destructive fears and detrimental thoughts when you feel discontent, attacked or criticised. Know that you can rise above anything that makes you feel frustrated.

An Indian couple brought me their five-year-old daughter. "We are at the end of our tether," they said. "She is a very obstinate and naughty child. She refuses to put on her school uniform and every morning we have the same struggle. It needs two of us to get her dressed. And look at her hair – she cut it off herself."

I used muscle testing on the child and the stress issue that came up was a fear of not being loved.

When I asked her to tell me who does not love her she burst into tears and exclaimed, "My mum and dad and my granny. They wanted me to be a boy and when I am big, they have to pay a lot of money when I get married."

I asked her what made her think this.

"My granny said so," she replied.

I then realised that there was a greater need for treatment of the parents than the child. I asked the parents into my therapy room without their daughter and I was told that she was the youngest of four girls. When I pointed out their daughter's distress they admitted to have been disappointed to have not had a boy. It was the parents' inability to adjust their expectations that caused the child's unhappiness and torment.

VERIFICATIONS AND AFFIRMATIONS

"I have no need to control others."

"I calm my mind and listen. I take things light and easy."

"I am nonjudgmental when I am pushed for challenge."

"My body, mind, spirit and emotions are balanced."

"I am full of vigour and let go of unnecessary worries."

"I nurture only positive thoughts."

"I am kind, tolerant, generous, skillful and wise with other people's points of view."

"I am flexible and enjoy being myself."

"I allow my relationship between my mind and body to flow freely."

"My problem is only in my mind."

"I am FREE to be ME!"

8. PATIENCE

"He that has patience may compass anything."

François Rabelais (1494-1553)

When things are going against you and your plans, do you feel that the whole world is against you?

When we lose patience, we lose control. This initiates hasty actions, which we may regret afterwards.

There is no benefit from taking by force what you would like to attain in a hurry. It is a wrong signal for courage and self-esteem.

There are no quick fixes to achieve patience.

To learn to be patient we need to be patient in our own struggle to learn the best way forward and how best to achieve our goals.

When you are under the pressure of time schedules, you need to learn to be calm and composed in order to find a platform that gives you inner balance. This is the only place for making the right decisions.

There is also another obstacle to surmount – to be open-minded with other people's ways when they cannot keep up with your speed and expectations. There is no need to 'hit the roof' when someone's actions challenge your patience. All that you achieve is insecurity in other people's competence and they will eventually lose their respect for you. Allow others some space to do their work in their own time. Learn to accept those who are slow to understand your way of working and use your vision to realise their potential.

Concentrate your feelings on being cheerful and supportive. Use your positive influence to encourage others and do not let your ambition get in your way. Then you give others the courage to be more able and efficient in their work.

When you have learned to accommodate other people's shortcomings, you can encourage them to be more confident and involved. You can then achieve better results by delegating those issues that get in the way of doing what you do best: using your expertise! This is called delegation and teamwork. Try and find the best way to deal with the options, one problem at a time. When delegating, you can always keep a distant eye to oversee the work you have passed on.

When we give way to inner turbulence – stress and too much push – we tend to hurry our steps and can easily misjudge those things that are meaningful to us. Learn to weigh up priorities.

Slow down a little and take control by practising the breathing exercises and tapping your thymus as described in Part II.

Allow some spare time and take a break to connect with nature, its treasures and its simplicity of life. Then, refreshed, you can return to your tasks and focus on those meaningful things suppressed by outside pressures.

My father had a saying, "Nach dem Essen soll man ruhn, oder tausend Schritte tun", to which he adhered religiously. It means after lunch have a rest or take a thousand steps.

Patience is a lesson for workaholics, always in a crisis, always running around. When you cannot see the wood for the trees you become a slave to your own irrational thoughts which will control you.

As with the quality of flexibility and balance allow each day at least half an hour for unforeseen circumstances, be it congested traffic or overwhelming demands and deadlines when you arrive at work etc.

Patience means disciplining yourself. Once you are at peace with yourself you can be in control, and you can install a fresh mind to your tasks ahead and be ready for the storm.

The wife of one of my patients made an appointment for her husband to see whether I could help to save their marriage.

"I can't cope with his constant agitation whenever I am around him, and he drinks too much," she told me on the phone prior to his appointment.

When I met this charming gentleman he looked calm and composed. As soon as he mentioned his wife, his manners changed and he became very agitated.

"She never listens when I speak to her and this makes me very angry and frustrated," he explained. "I have learned to go my own way. Whenever I want to share a new idea with her I hit a blank expression and this makes me feel very restricted in whatever I want to do. I seem to easily lose my temper which may also be the reason why I make many wrong decisions in my business. If only I could be less stressed and more patient."

He was on various drugs from his doctor for high blood pressure, a stomach ulcer, a diaphragmatic hernia and depression.

I learned that he had been sent to boarding school at the age of eight where he had to obey rules and felt very isolated. We started by working on his suppressed and unresolved feelings that he put away as a young boy and he admitted that he was never allowed to be who he wanted to be. He had to learn to disengage himself from his feelings, his needs and so he felt very lonely.

Once he got married, he found himself in the same predicament with his wife and explained, "She doesn't understand me".

We worked on him learning to trust himself and others and not to feel inadequate while at the same time being open and patient enough to allow the other person to express their views and feelings in their own time.

In one of the sessions, we worked on self-love and self-understanding. Then I gave him some breathing exercises to practise and the quality section on patience with various affirmations.

His wife phoned me soon afterwards to tell me, "I don't know what you have done, but my husband is much more relaxed and we can have a proper conversation with each other without him shouting at me."

So remember, a lack of patience can lead to loneliness and weak decision-making!

VERIFICATIONS AND AFFIRMATIONS

"I now step away from judging others and learn to listen."

"I am comfortable and tolerant with myself and towards others."

"I am in control of my emotions, and concentrate on appreciating the simplicity of life."

"I am calm and serene. I am always open to learning."

"I now release all hard thoughts and pride. I share only positive emotions with others."

"I calm my nerves and emotional tensions."

"I have respect and patience with others."

"I am always clear and focused. I am able to listen to others even if they are slow to understand and so challenge my patience."

"I am tolerant and express myself without being angry."

"I allow myself to go with the flow. I am secure. I enjoy each moment. I am adaptable to change."

"I am FREE to be ME!"

9. BEINGNESS

"And let today embrace the past with remembrance and the future with longing. You are good when you are one with yourself."

The Prophet Kahlil Gibran (1883-1931)

Beingness means to use all your inner mastering to be yourself and let others be and not try to control them.

When life around you is in chaos and the patterns of the fabric of your life become distorted, you need extra vigilance to allow others to be. Respect that they have their own life's struggles to deal with.

Furthermore, this quality becomes a challenge when you are without inner guidance and you are not connected to your true self.

Simply ask yourself:

- "Who am I?"
- "What is the future path I would like to follow?"

Now consider this:

- "Why do I do the things other people pressurise me to do?"
- "Why am I always running to other people's insistent demands?"

Recognise the point where you stop the flow and are unable to function by NOT being.

When you are in tune with your true inner self and with what you believe is a meaningful life, you do not need to justify your actions, nor criticise others anymore. Simply stay with your feelings and allow yourself to be.

Practise saying no when you feel it is right and do not be afraid to say what you want to say. It is all about communication by making statements of your own opinion. This way others know where you are.

At the same time do not criticise others. When criticism comes your way, listen carefully, and take a moment to contemplate before you answer. Then apply assertive communication skills; this means without being judgemental.

Stay positive in your thoughts and have faith in your decisive discernment. This will empower you to support your true thoughts and intentions. At the same time understand and accept that there is nothing much you can do or change for the moment.

Simply believe in yourself and do not let other people's opinions affect your potential. At the same time, never lose sight of your aspirations. You need to allow room for positive thinking, fun and joy and not become a hard taskmaster of yourself in order to accomplish your ambitions.

When life's demands overwhelm you, declutter and work out what is right and what is wrong in your life. Then consider making some changes to those activities that are priorities and have meaning.

Step away from obsessive thinking and become more being. Stay in tune with life and being yourself. If you touch others with optimism the positive energy that flows out from you is the greatest offering you can share with others.

A pale-looking seventeen-year-old boy came to see me. He sat with his legs crossed and his hands tightly clasped together, so much so that his knuckles turned white with pressure.

"How can I help?" I asked.

After a little while he whispered, "I have heard you on the radio."

Then after shifting his body a few times, he added, "I can't go out by myself, because I can't cross a road. I can't do anything without my mother interfering."

When I asked him how he got to my clinic, he replied, "I allowed myself a lot of time to get here."

Muscle testing indicated that he needed a stress-release in health kinesiology. I found that his meridian system was blocked and I had to hold many of his acupuncture points while he repeated, "I am afraid of being confined and constrained."

His arms and legs started to jerk as we progressed with releasing this stress.

After the treatment he told me that when he was two years old, his father died in a road accident when crossing a road. From then on his mother became overprotective of him. "I was never allowed to ride a bicycle or go out and play with friends. Whenever I went to school my mother would accompany me and, to my embarrassment, always held my hand when we had to cross a road."

We worked on his self-assurance and self-confidence using health kinesiology and, on leaving, I gave him a bottle of Rescue Remedy to take just before his next visit and this affirmation:

"I have the confidence and willpower to do everything I want to do. I am important and value myself."

When he left the clinic, the colour had returned to his face. He improved further after each session, so much so that, after the third visit, he felt well and confident. One month later, he popped in briefly to tell me that he had

had an unfortunate encounter with a sign that fell down from the front of a bank and hit him on the head, knocking him to the ground. "I calmly got up and just laughed, then proceeded to cross the main road."

Beingness also means to open up your heart to nature – a unique gift we often take for granted.

To sum up, beingness means to let go of obsessive thinking and be in tune with yourself and your belief system. Respect others and the world around you, no matter what obstacles or criticism frustrate you.

Simply be. Believe in your own power and at the same time do not isolate yourself from others and nature.

This is the essence of beingness.

VERIFICATIONS AND AFFIRMATIONS

"I allow myself to be inspired."

"I am filled with inspiration for my future."

"I now relax and am in control."

"I am positive and self-confident and in charge of my own life."

"I trust in the universe and now create the right attitude to move onwards in my life."

"I no longer need to be restrained or have to demonstrate my power."

"I will practise saying no once a day to trivial things."

"I easily let go of all petty patterns and now rise above all the things that get in my way."

"I believe in myself and do not let other people's judgement affect my potential. No one has the power to contort or harass my life's path."

"I live in the now and circulate easily with the flow of life."

"I am FREE to be ME!"

10. FREEDOM

"There is no such thing as part-freedom.

"To be free is not merely to cast off one's chains, but to live in a way that respects and enhances the lives of others.

"Freedom is not only the opportunity to vote, but the gate to the awareness of many problems: hunger, poverty, illness, non-advancement."

Nelson Mandela

"You are responsible for your life" is an expression often conveyed to us by enlightened authors. "Just change your thoughts, accept your shortcomings and difficulties and stay positive. Learn to be in control of your life – it is no problem; simply change your thoughts."

Easier said than done. What if the husband is unemployed, the roof is leaking and the bills are unpaid?

What if our health is failing us? Most of us are completely unaware that the first symptoms of pain or feeling unwell could be due to unresolved stress issues.

When you are down or are suffering from ill health, did it occur to you to stop and question yourself: "When did my depression or health problems start? Did I have family or relationship difficulties, an argument with friends or suffer rejection at work? Could this be the reason I have fallen ill? Could it be that these difficulties place a burden on my happiness and freedom?" Then ask yourself further, "What lesson can I learn from this? What is it teaching me? How can I move forward when everything is on top of me and I cannot change the way I feel or act?"

Try and reflect on your childhood years. Although circumstances may have been different then, do you have similar unpleasant feelings now?

In my work I find that, when a person is carrying unresolved childhood emotions or fears, these feelings can reappear in later life when the person can be affected by the same fear or negative emotion, although they might find themselves in different circumstances. By then they have become deep-seated and buried in the subconscious, which affects the body's energies.

Some people go through life unable to truly see who they are, what their life's purpose is and why they can't speak up for themselves. I have met many such unfortunate souls. Our body signals to us in various ways. Most of us are completely unaware that, by ignoring the first symptoms of feeling unwell, we stop the natural flow of our life energies that could be our bodies sending out a cry for help.

Whenever we cannot handle stress in our daily lives, the body's natural flow of energies is being suppressed. If we continue to override our body's tolerance it can no longer keep up with our commands. Without realising, we get swept away into the continually demanding pace of everyday life and live constantly on adrenal overload. We are sucked into today's ever increasing kaleidoscope of working life. The speed in which we operate nowadays is dictated by our survival mode which tells us that we have to be always up to date with the newest technological advances.

We strive to be constantly one step ahead and to stay in control in order to perform. This pressure to work at one's utmost can creep in gradually and is on the increase. Yet, we are so busy living that we shut off contact with our inner self. We become totally unable to listen to our body's cries.

At first it might be just a niggling painful knee, tension in the neck and shoulders, digestive disorders, a sudden outbreak of a skin rash or even panic attacks.

Most patients I see at this stage have usually put up with their little aches and pains, but come to seek help when their symptoms worsen. They expect me to remove their discomforts there and then, preferably by administering a remedy that treats all symptoms at once! When muscle testing reveals some hidden stressors that need to be addressed first, the patient often becomes quite surprised, "What has stress got to do with my health problems?"

A very attractive lady came to see me. "I hope that you can help me. I have been suffering from constipation all my life."

I prescribed a herbal remedy for her. Muscle testing indicated that she also needed a stress release. I used health kinesiology and found this issue: she feared that things would happen beyond her control. She was quite surprised at this but allowed me to go ahead. During the treatment she fell asleep and her temperature dropped. She felt cold and I covered her up with a blanket.

Afterwards, on reflection, she suddenly realised that, apart from business travels abroad, she never went on holiday. Although she fell pregnant and gave birth to a lovely daughter, she never married. She also declined to take on the top job in her career. I used my psychic energy to find out more about this issue and I saw her as a little baby of seven months old in the womb.

The following day my patient asked her mother whether she remembered a foreboding or fear at that time of her pregnancy. After taking some time to reflect, she phoned her daughter.

She remembered, "When I was about seven months pregnant with you, your father was a soldier at the

Normandy landings and I hadn't heard from him for a month. Every time I heard some footsteps on our gravel path I felt terrified in case someone was coming to give me bad news."

Some months later I met this lady again. She told me that her bowel movements had become more regular and asked for a repeat prescription of one of my special bowel tonics. She had also been on her first holiday away from England and enjoyed every minute of it! "I have also started making plans to set up my own business; something I have always dreamt of but never had the courage to seriously consider."

Wouldn't it be great to pack our bags, leave all the worries behind and start life somewhere else again? Even if you could afford to do this, remember that you may take your old unresolved baggage with you!

Freedom starts when you can nurture only positive thoughts, and enjoy inner stillness, gratitude, contentment and love and care for yourself and others.

Take your first step to freedom today.

Start to function by stimulating your actions and opening your doors to new experiences. Take the courage and look at yourself clearly.

Ask yourself:

- "What is it I am missing most in my life?"
- "Do I avoid facing the real world?"
- "When did I stop to look at myself?"
- "How can I enrich my life?"
- "Is my attitude such that nothing can be done?"
- "Do I allow my life to pass me by?"

- "What is the purpose of my life?"

- "What am I really passionate about?"

- "Is it really such a big deal to pick up the pieces and to make changes for my own good, however small?"

You can achieve freedom when you are comfortable with yourself; when you are forgiving and allow others the freedom to pursue their own.

Once you have a clear goal in mind and dare to step beyond your comfort zone, you will find that it is no big deal to bring about wonderful new changes you never thought were within your reach. Start by giving yourself the time and space to enjoy the simple things in life. They don't have to be expensive. A walk in the park, smelling the roses – simply feeling alive!

Also practise and master the affirmations and self-help items described in Part II. They are designed to invigorate your energy.

Freedom is when you can release fear and let go of hurt. Then you will be able to invigorate your energy and see your life's drama unfolding clearly.

VERIFICATIONS AND AFFIRMATIONS

"I am comfortable with myself and I trust and value myself."

"I always keep a positive attitude and trust the universe."

"I greet every day with optimism, joy and ease. I see every day as a new beginning."

"'I feel safe and protect myself and am always ready to learn and nurture myself."

"I am relaxed and focused on new ideas and opportunities."

"I create harmony and am in touch with my inner beautiful self and connect with nature."

"I allow my body to be free from past emotional scarring and worries. I know that I am safe and can create my very own personal space."

"My life's experiences are my teachers."

"I am calm. I am responsible. I am adequate. I am humble and understanding. I am full of gratitude."

"Life is good! Love is good!"

"I am FREE to be ME!"

EFFECTIVE GOAL SETTING

At first you might think that your present situation in life is hopeless. However, you never know what is just around the corner. There is always hope for you. Setting your goals will help you to make changes to achieve personal evolution and fulfilment in your life.

With the help of the Ten Qualities you can:

- teach yourself courage and love
- have a better understanding of yourself
- build new bridges to wholeness
- dare to face your limitations and struggles and so help yourself to move beyond your boundaries
- turn your limitations and your life's struggles inside out to help you deal with safe boundaries and to move on.

Some of us live 'unlived' lives because we make too many excuses or hold too many negative attitudes. We deal only with what we know and shut down instead of living through stagnation or painful memories.

You have the power to change. Start by honouring and respecting yourself and your relationships.

Open up to your wisdom within and be open to opportunities that present themselves; accept what is blocking or repressing you.

You will find that by writing your goals down in your exercise book, you will feel a sense of relief. The **intent** alone can change into positive energy! Then be bold and move beyond your comfort zone with a willingness to take action. Think of your own needs and what you can reasonably achieve. The word *mañana* (tomorrow) does not serve you well if you want to venture out and succeed.

Effective goal setting starts by communicating with your biocomputer – your conscious brain. Prepare yourself for the future. Start by upgrading your programming by putting the power of yourself into action and ask yourself:

- "Which of my goals are realistic, clear and positive?"

- "Which of my goals best supports and helps me with my life's purpose?"

Before you continue, say the following affirmations **aloud**:

- -"I accept myself as a beautiful person. I am loving and lovable."

- "I feel good about myself."

- "My body is ready to learn new skills."

- "I have the courage to understand myself and I am now creating a new and exciting bridge to wholeness."

- "I release all past unhappy mental and emotional states."

- "I am now upgrading my performance by releasing all 'toxic' effects that, until now, have prevented me from achieving my future functioning."

- "I now tap into the richness of my meaningful thoughts to realise my dreams."

- "I am ready to learn new skills easily."

- "I now give myself permission to proceed and move beyond my life's repressions for a NEW ME!"

Should any of the above affirmations feel uncomfortable or somewhat alien for you to say aloud, I suggest that you might like to repeat these three times a day for one week before moving on to the next chapter. The same applies to the affirmations in the Ten Qualities. A good way to say affirmations is to look into your eyes in a mirror. You could also put a tune to your affirmations and sing them whole-heartedly.

SHORT-TERM GOALS

To start this process, jot down some short-term goals in a journal and some actions you plan to take to manifest them.

SHORT-TERM GOALS	
1	
2	
3	
4	
5	

ACTIONS	
1	
2	
3	
4	
5	

3- TO 5-YEAR PLAN

If you wish to strive for a greater challenge, it might be helpful to construct a 3- or 5-year plan for each goal using this template:

LIST YOUR GOAL HERE	
1st year: what preparations do I need to achieve this year?	
1	
2	
3	
2nd year: what needs my work and full attention during this year?	
1	
2	
3	
3rd year: to accomplish my goal in five years' time, what are my next endeavours in order to make it happen?	
1	
2	
3	

Be aware: you might get what you want!

PART 2
YOUR SELF-HELP
TOOLS

THE POWER OF WORDS

We can affect the way we feel, think or do by just changing one tiny word. This gives us a simple way to enhance the level of our performance

Words have great power both when spoken and when running inside our heads. Our world is generated by our thoughts. All we need to do therefore is change our thoughts for the world to become a kinder, more magical place.

Of course, we all have free will and we can choose whether we believe this or not. Irrespective of your beliefs, it's free to give it a go.

Overleaf, the column on the left shows common words that attract negativity. However, if we pay attention to what we are saying and use positive statements, we can improve profoundly the way we do things and how we feel about them.

Try it and see – it works like magic!

I have to	I choose to
I will try	I will do my best
I have a problem	I have an opportunity
I hope	I will
I should	I can
I should be more positive	I am positive
I wish	I want
But	And
I am not good at...	I am having a go at this I am getting better at this
I can't do this	I do my best
I am sure I will mess this up	I do my best to make a good job of this
I have got to do...	I am happy to do...

THE THYMUS GLAND

The thymus gland is situated approximately five centimetres below the notch where the collarbones meet, behind the centre of the sternum (breastbone) in the adult body.

It signified heart, life, soul and desire for the Ancient Greeks.

Consider these three statements defining what we know about the function of the thymus gland from three perspectives.

Statement 1

The Collins English Dictionary (1997) defines the thymus as follows: 'A glandular organ of vertebrates, consisting in man of two lobes situated below the thyroid. It atrophies with age and it is almost non-existent in the adult.'

Statement 2

In the 'Synopsis of Applied Kinesiology', Dr. George Goodheart observed that: "Until recently the thymus gland was very much overlooked in the adult. When thymus and parotid substances were placed in the mouth together, weak muscles associated with the endocrine system strengthened."

Statement 3

Back in 1979, Dr. John Diamond explored the function of the thymus gland further via kinesiological muscle testing. He discovered that this gland controls life energy in the body, or what many healers refer to as chi, qi, life force or vital energy.

I recommend reading his book 'Your Body Doesn't Lie', especially for the skeptic!

Dr. Diamond also found that the thymus gland still holds childhood emotions. Furthermore, he demonstrated that, by using muscle testing, the thymus gland reduces in energy in response to stress.

Once the stress is removed, the muscle response when touching the thymus gland tests strong.

He could confirm, again via muscle testing, that there is a link between the mind and body and how the thymus gland is the first organ affected by stress and mental attitudes.

He also states that "a healthy, active thymus gland makes for vibrant and positive health".

Whenever he found emotional blockages or disease processes, the thymus gland tested weak and he concluded that "there is an immediate reduction of life energy".

Furthermore, he undertook muscle testing of over 30,000 musical recordings on students and could verify via muscle feedback testing that certain composers could stimulate and enhance life energy.

During my own studies in anatomy and physiology I learned that the thymus is an intricate system involving many functions, e.g. it secretes special T-cells (T is for thymus) and lymphocytes to support the immune system responses.

I also learned that the thymus gland has no further function in adults once the growth processes have been completed. This was thirty years ago.

Recent research of the thymus has been linked to the hypothalamus – our master gland (like a *chef d'orchestre*) – and that the thymus gland is thought to be directly linked to brain processes.

Various connections have since been made between the nervous and immune system and how the mind can influence susceptibility to disease. The findings of a network of nerve endings found in the thymus gland may explain this theory.

I remember taking my children to a zoo. When we approached the monkey enclosure, a huge gorilla looked at us and started to hit his chest vigorously. Primal reflexes? Maybe we could learn from the behaviour of animals?

When a 62-year-old gentleman came to see me, I asked whether he would allow me to test his 'life energy'. He was recently made redundant and was put on heavy antidepressants by his doctor. "Just do what you think might help me. My wife cannot deal with my negative state and I am worried she might leave me."

I have an amazing piece of equipment called ACMOS (as mentioned on page 19). It allows me to ascertain very quickly if there are blockages in our energy field.

So I took out my ACMOS equipment and tested the energy in his acupuncture meridians.

Then I asked him to tap his thymus gland a few times. On retesting I found that some of his meridians had increased in energy!

So thank you, John Diamond, for putting the thymus gland back on the map and pointing out that the conventional wisdom of statement 1 should be reassessed.

HOW TO ENHANCE YOUR THYMUS ENERGY

Whenever you feel harassed or stressed, tapping the thymus gland can help greatly. Just 20 taps is all it needs and you can use it for the following:

- to balance and harmonise your body's energies
- to enhance your immune system (e.g. if you feel the onset of a cold or flu)
- to heighten your stamina and vitality
- to give yourself a creative boost when you are flagging
- to protect yourself from people's negative energies around you
- if you are overwhelmed by too many responsibilities.

Note that even just by breathing properly, the thymus gland seems to be activated by means of movement of the respiratory muscles.

Thymus Tapping

So, sit quietly and slow down your breathing.

When you feel relaxed, slightly bend four fingers of one hand inwards to meet up with your bent thumb and place it over the thymus area. Then place the other hand, palms down, over your navel.

Now use your bent fingers and thumb to tap lightly over the thymus area, as if you are tapping against an egg without breaking the shell.

Do this about 20 times, or using 3 to 4 small breaths is sufficient.

I often resort to this 'thymus tap' whenever I've had a long day at work or after seeing a 'difficult patient'.

You might find that this is often followed by a deep sigh.

Location of the thymus

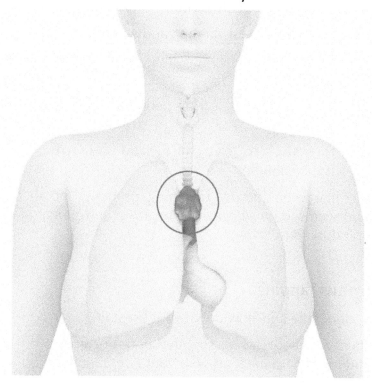

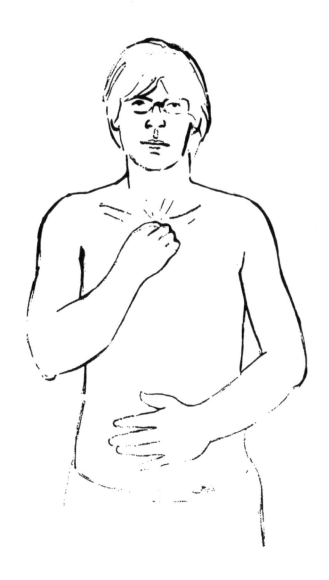

MUSCLE TESTING

Muscle testing is an art and, like all arts, needs practice for you to become confident and perfect.

Muscle testing was first developed by Dr. George Goodheart, an American chiropractor and the creator of applied kinesiology. It is taught at Touch for Health seminars and can be carried out by laypeople with no clinical background.

Muscle testing requires two people. The person who is testing is referred to below as the **tester** and the person being tested I like to call the **testee**.

Both the tester and the testee need to have a positive attitude and be interested in the discovery and outcome of a muscle test. Muscle testing can be done standing, sitting or lying down. When sitting or lying down, ensure that the testee's legs are not crossed.

The most important thing to keep in mind when you do muscle testing is that it is not a contest of strength! When we perform a muscle test we test the integrity of the response of a muscle and NOT how strong you or the other person is.

Before starting the muscle test both the tester and testee should read through the instructions below to become more familiar as to what the test involves. Both of you should drink a glass of water to help the energy flow.

This is the procedure for muscle testing whilst standing:

Before starting the muscle test, the tester should always ask the testee for permission to test.

The tester should lightly tap his/her and the testee's thymus.

Both the tester and testee stand upright, opposite each other, in a relaxed position with both feet slightly apart. Then the tester takes a small step to his/her left so as not to block the testee's central meridian energy flow. This keeps the midline meridian of the testee unobstructed.

The tester should then ask the testee to hold out their left arm straight in front, parallel to the floor and then ask them to move it outwards to the side (see illustration) with the thumb and fingers relaxed.

The tester then places two fingers above the wrist on the outstretched arm of the testee and lightly places the thumb of the same hand below the two fingers underneath the wrist without applying too much pressure. The thumb is merely for support.

Too much pressure of the thumb can affect the meridian flow of the testee's wrist (we have six meridians travelling past each wrist). The other hand of the tester is placed on top of the opposite shoulder, simply to be used as a stabiliser for the person being tested.

The tester should explain and demonstrate that the range of movement of the muscle being tested (the deltoid muscle which caps the shoulder) is simply a downward action and to resist when the command 'hold' is given.

Now we begin to muscle test. The tester needs to keep his/her mind blank while testing. Then the tester gives a verbal command of "hold" or "resist". Now the tester relaxes the thumb and concentrates on the fingers above the wrist.

The tester needs to wait for 2 seconds before applying a downward pressure slowly. The muscle should be able to respond within 1½ to 2 inches when pushing the arm down. The tester needs to maintain this pressure for two seconds to verify the response. The muscle should stay strong. If the testee's response is weak, the test can be repeated and the testee can be asked to resist slightly more than before.

If the muscle stays strong, the body's energies have not changed. If the muscle tests weak, the tester should try the other arm of the testee. If for any reason the muscle testing is not conclusive, the test can be performed again after tapping both the tester and testee's thymus.

After testing, the tester should always help the testee's arm back to the side of the body with the help of the thumb as a support. Trust the result of the muscle response.

If this testing procedure is unsuccessful, the testee's 'left side/right side' brain may be 'switched'. I recommend performing a Cross Crawl exercise (see under Exercises for Well-Being) and then repeat the muscle testing as before.

Muscle responses can also be practiced by drawing a plus sign on a clean white sheet of paper. When the testee looks at the plus sign during a muscle test, the arm should stay strong. Then draw a minus sign. When looking at a minus sign, then the muscle should test weak.

The simple rule is: '2 seconds', i.e. wait 2 seconds after saying "hold" or "resist" before starting the muscle test. Allow 2 seconds of downward movement (note that the arm should not move more than 1½ to 2 inches.

Allow 2 seconds' holding time in the locked position; to verify the response, the arm should hold strong. (Do not bounce the arm up and down when testing).

Once you are comfortable with your testing procedure, you are ready to test for the Ten Qualities. Note, whenever I teach beginners how to muscle test in my Touch for Health seminars, I come equipped with a letter-weighing scale. I ask each student to visualise the strength needed for accurate muscle testing and to perform a muscle test on the scale. It is interesting to find that almost all students apply anywhere between 1kg to 3kg of weight!

Only 250g or less of pressure is necessary in order to get an accurate muscle feedback response without overpowering the muscle. Note that I use approximately 100g or less of pressure and remember we test only the energy response of the muscle.

My definition of a weak muscle response, like the arm giving way, does not mean that the actual muscle being tested becomes weak. It simply means that the integrity of the muscle's energy has been challenged for a brief moment, to give information as feedback of how the body responds to incoming information.

HOW TO TEST FOR THE TEN QUALITIES

Overleaf you will find a listing of all the Ten Qualities.

Assuming that you are the tester; ask the testee to place a finger on the first quality of Enjoyment. Then perform a muscle test on the testee's other arm. If the arm gives way you have found a quality the testee needs to learn about.

A weak muscle response indicates that Enjoyment, for example, affects the body's energy.

Next go to the verifications and affirmation page on Enjoyment in Part 1 and test each number to find which affirmation is the best to do.

Always finish with "I am FREE to be Me" after the affirmation.

If the muscle tests strong on enjoyment, move on to the next quality and so on.

Incidentally, you can also test for which of the self-help tools the testee would benefit from. To do this, muscle test using the list of Exercises for Well Being, also overleaf.

You might find at first that too much muscle testing can make the testee's muscle tired. If this happens, simply use the other arm or have a break.

Muscle testing is a true biofeedback system from the body.

It is easy, non-invasive, safe and fun! Practice, of course, makes perfect!

TESTING FOR THE TEN QUALITIES

Enjoyment

Giving, gratitude and humility

Creativity and fulfilment

Responsibility and consideration

Confidence and trust

Detachment

Flexibility and balance

Patience

Beingness

Freedom

TESTING FOR EXERCISES FOR WELL-BEING

Cross Crawling

Brain Gym: Focus Points

Calming and Centring Exercise

The 'Stress Aspirin'

The Importance and Significance of Posture

How to Check Your Posture

Daily Postural Awareness Check

The Vitality of Water

Breathing Exercise

The Learning Tree

The Healing Tree

Choose Your Healing Tree

Exercising

Salute to the Sun

EXERCISES FOR WELL-BEING

Waiting until you become ill until you do something is like waiting for your car to go wrong before giving it a service.

Here's a set of simple things you can do to help yourself, your family and your friends.

They are infectious, in a nice way, so do spread the word.

CROSS CRAWL

Duration: approx. 20 seconds

Cross Crawl is helpful in stimulating the flow of cerebrospinal fluid (CSF), which is a clear alkaline fluid that surrounds the brain and spinal cord.

Stagnation of CSF can result in impaired communication within the brain. When cranial bones get stuck together, this fluid does not get pumped well into the spinal cord and so can cause muscle weakness with the result of a one-sided imbalance and faulty energy communication across the body.

The dichotomy of left side/right side brain function is seen as follows:

- the left brain relates to the verbal, logical, rational, mathematical, masculine and negative
- the right brain deals with the non-logical, non-sensible, non-practical, intuitive, feminine and positive.

Recent research indicates that the left brain works inside space and time and the right brain, everywhere and 'everywhen' else.

It is worth mentioning here that, although you may be a well-balanced left/right brain operator, when you are affected by allergies the brain can react with 'cross switching'.

This can cause adrenal and pancreatic interaction as well as mental and emotional misinformation and confusion. If you think you are suffering from allergies or food intolerances you could seek a Touch for Health practitioner to test you.

Benefits of Cross Crawl:

- Helps to stimulate the flow of vital CSF and lymph
- Encourages the neurological organisation of the brain-crossing effect between left and right hemispheres of the brain
- Improves concentration and learning abilities
- Improves coordination
- Is helpful with dyslexia problems
- Reduces stress and tension in the body
- Increases energy

Cross Crawl is usually practised standing and is simply an exaggerated walking movement by moving the opposite arm and leg at the same time whilst remaining on the same spot – see the drawing below. At the same time, look ahead and focus on a non-moving object. About twenty sets of movements can be beneficial, but do NOT count them. If you have coordination problems you might like to perform this exercise with someone near you in case you lose your balance! After two days you will find that this exercise becomes easier.

Whenever you go for a walk, relax your body and move your arms freely.

There are many variations of Cross Crawl that are taught in educational kinesiology (Edu-K) and Brain Gym. However, you might like to add the following:

Once you are comfortable with the basic exercise, you could proceed with some eye movements. Continue with the Cross Crawl, then move your eyes to look up to the left, by again focusing them upon a non-moving point, whilst still keeping your head facing forward. After a few movements, say ten sets or so, look down to the right.

Throughout this exercise keep your head absolutely still and always facing ahead. Finish by doing the Cross Crawl a few more times with the eyes looking straight ahead.

By using eye movements, we exaggerate the transfer of information from the left to the right brain via the corpus callosum. This can be imagined as a telephone exchange between our left brain (the analytical) and our right brain (the creational, emotional). This can reroute some of the brain's switching system, especially when we are stressed and cannot concentrate. Extremely useful before exams or interviews!

Babies should be encouraged to crawl for some time before they walk. This crawling stage is extremely important in the neurological patterning of left/right brain as it later relates to speech and reading skills.

The parent can do this exercise with the baby lying on its back and gently moving each arm in turn towards its opposite leg. It can be great fun for the baby if at the same time you can sing or say a nursery rhyme, keeping to a steady rhythm.

One of our healthiest holidays was when we went cross-country skiing in Canada and also in the Black Forest in Germany. In the latter resort, they even had floodlit tracks for those who wanted to go for an evening outing before dinner. You simply placed your skis into specially prepared tracks and, without any effort, followed the prepared path. This resulted in us treating ourselves with the purchase of our own cross-country skis.

Whenever we are blessed with a light snowfall in Surrey, we put on our skis and enjoy ourselves, and so replenish our energies, by naturally doing the Cross Crawl at the same time.

CROSS CRAWL IS FUN !

BRAIN GYM: FOCUS POINTS

(Duration: 2-10 minutes)

Whenever your mind is in overdrive and you find it difficult to focus on an important matter, these points can be very useful in helping you to concentrate.

Find a quiet space and sit comfortably with both legs slightly apart. Place the fingertips of both your hands together to form a circle. Then start to breathe gently. As you breathe in, visualise your breath moving up from the base of your spine to the top and when you exhale, guide your breath slowly back to where you started.

Then hold your Focus Points by placing one hand gently over your forehead and the other one at the back of the head (see illustration). It does not matter which hand goes where – just do whatever is comfortable. Focus on your priority issue. Whenever there is too much 'mind-chatter' going on, simply send it away and persevere, whilst continuing your breathing.

Some time ago I attended a workshop in kinesiology with Gordon Stokes, entitled 'Where is Your Focus?' The aim of the seminar was to use that part of us that knows everything about us: the subconscious brain.

He asked us to think of ourselves as powerful magnets. "Let your thoughts reach out to bring to you that which you continually dwell upon."

He then warned us, "Be careful of what you wish for because you may get what you want."

He also explained that we perform according to our self-image influenced by parents, teachers, friends, fears and experiences. He showed us how we can defuse our patterned self-image and how to perform with an eye to 'seeing' clearly; to express our personal and emotional intentions by way of focus, intention and imagination.

True, we don't trust our feelings enough. We know best, yet preprogrammed feelings get in our way. By denying emotions we cut off our power. Our belief system dictates our self-image from which we make choices about the way we act, dress and what we want.

Gordon shared with us his 'cowboys with the crops' story.

When he was young, he wanted to help the cowboys bring in the crops, but his father told him that he was too small. He sat on the doorstep and cried.

When his grandfather asked him why he was crying he told him that he was too young to work with the cowboys, to which his grandfather replied, "Cowboys never cry."

From then on he never cried. By denying his emotions, he became cut off from his power and any readiness to change. From then on he suppressed his emotions and became tense until he came across kinesiology. This opened up a new world for him and he learned how to get in touch with his emotions again. How we are programmed in any time can change our future actions and reactions.

Now it was time for the class to get to work. Gordon asked us to hold our Focus Points and think of something that we really wanted or what annoyed us continually. Having recently set up my holistic clinic, my thoughts went immediately to an upset I suffered quietly, on entering one of my clinic treatment rooms.

One of my therapists had stuck creased-up posters on my newly decorated walls, advertising pillows for sale, which had nothing to do with the therapy he used. I didn't have the heart to confront him but got more and more angry with myself for not speaking up.

Whilst holding my Focus Points, an image presented itself to me. In my mind I saw clearly that I was holding a bunch of pencils in black and white.

Then I remembered that when I was five years old on the first day of school, we were given pictures to colour in. My choice of colouring pencils was limited to only five in a small plastic packet.

Next to me sat a farmer's boy who proudly opened up his enormous box of colouring pencils. I asked him whether I could borrow the purple one. He told me that he needed it.

I patiently waited until he was bored of using it and, reluctantly, he passed it on to me. I was very excited and began by carefully filling in the hat of the Easter bunny in my picture. I still remember the smooth touch of the soft tip and the deep purple.

Suddenly, this boy snatched it away from me, which caused a nasty smudge all across my picture, and told me that I could not use it any more. I then found myself watching him for the rest of the lesson, longing to try some of the other colouring pencils that he wasn't using. I knew my parents could never afford to buy them for me.

Whilst holding my Focus Points I felt very tearful. I soldiered on by holding my points when, all of a sudden, I saw an image in my mind: the pencils I was holding had turned into a display of vibrant colours. I had what I wanted. It goes without saying that two days later, when I met up with this therapist, I had a word and asked him to take down the offending posters. Every time since, whenever I felt overwhelmed by responsibility and my workload, I walk down the corridor from my room to the reception, proudly holding my colouring pencils!

"Thought occupies itself with past and future; once freed of both, the obstacle is vanquished."

Jajaluddin Rumi

CALMING AND CENTRING EXERCISE

(Duration: approx. 2 minutes)

The following exercise is based on the Tibetan figure of eight energy flow. In Tibetan medicine it is understood that subsidiary energy flows in circles of a figure of eight pattern along the front and back of the body. This does not relate to meridian energy flow. Whenever the physical body is under stress, the figure of eight energy can get disturbed.

Benefits of the exercise:

- better joint mobility

- less physical pain

- creates a sense of calm

Balancing exercise

Find a quiet place and sit comfortably in an upright position with both feet on the floor. Now place both hands together with all the fingertips touching (see Figure on page 108) and take a few gentle breaths.

Now bring your left foot over your right knee and let the left ankle rest over your right knee. Then move your right arm down towards the left foot and place your hand over the top of your left foot with the fingertips underneath it. The left arm reaches down alongside the inside of the left foot with the palm facing the other hand, so that the fingertips of both hands are touching (see Figure on page 109). Adjust your posture, relax your shoulders and sit quietly.

(You can also start with the opposite foot and hands, if more comfortable).

When you exhale, open your mouth and relax your tongue. Concentrate on your body's energies. Do not inhale too much air or you could become dizzy. You might like to do this for about a minute or so.

Then follow by placing your feet back on the floor and finish by resting your hands on your lap or midway up your body, whatever feels right for you, with all fingertips gently touching each other. Hold this position for about a minute, or continue as long as it feels comfortable. During this posture resume normal breathing.

This exercise was demonstrated to me by Wayne Cook, a kinesiologist, and has since been referred to as the Wayne Cook Posture. He uses this exercise as part of other techniques for treating dyslexia, learning difficulties and stuttering. This exercise is part of Brain Gym, taught at Edu-K (Educational Kinesiology).

Caution: Should the first stage of the above exercise cause discomfort, e.g. back pain, it is best not to do this exercise and see an osteopath, chiropractor or Touch for Health practitioner to check your muscle tone.

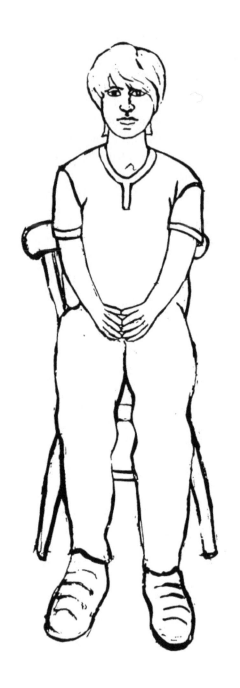

'STRESS ASPIRIN'

(Duration: anything between 5 and 15 minutes)

Use this whenever you are suffering from tension headaches, sleeplessness or if you have experienced an unpleasant occurrence, be it a stressful situation at work or at home, or if you find it difficult to deal with a bereavement.

Encouraged by his findings and through his insight and intensive research, Dr. Goodheart came across neurovascular reflex points. They were originally discovered in the 1930s by a chiropractor, Dr Terence Bennett.

Dr Bennett found specific areas, situated mainly on the head and some on the body, which he felt were influencing the vascularity of various structures and bodily functions. With the use of X-rays he could determine a change in blood flow to the body, depending on application of firm or light pressure to these points. He also noted a slight pulsation when applying a light touch with his fingertips to these areas.

These pulses are known not to be related to the heartbeat and usually work at a steady rate of 70-74 beats per minute. They also seem to be influenced by the flow of cerebrospinal fluid, believed to be affected by microscopic movements of the cranial bones during breathing. Muscle weakness can be caused if these bones in the skull become slightly stuck together, thus causing the flow of the fluid to be impeded rather than pumped freely through the spinal column.

Neurovascular holding points can be invaluable in helping you to calm down and gain control over your emotions and in rebuilding your stamina. This is especially useful for children who are upset and unhappy.

To begin, find a quiet place and tap your thymus.

The neurovascular points you want to use are found on the forehead, in line with the pupils and midway between the eyebrows and natural hairline.

Slightly bend your fingers and place them lightly over these points, then gently stretch the skin upwards with your fingertips without asserting pressure. You may be aware of a pulsing sensation below your fingertips, but do not worry if at first you are unable to feel the pulses.

Next focus on the subject that causes you distress whilst continually holding your points lightly. This can sometimes take one to five minutes or more.

During the treatment, you might find that the holding points pulsate unevenly. You must persevere until the pulses are synchronised.

You can either hold these points yourself or apply them on another person, of course with their permission.

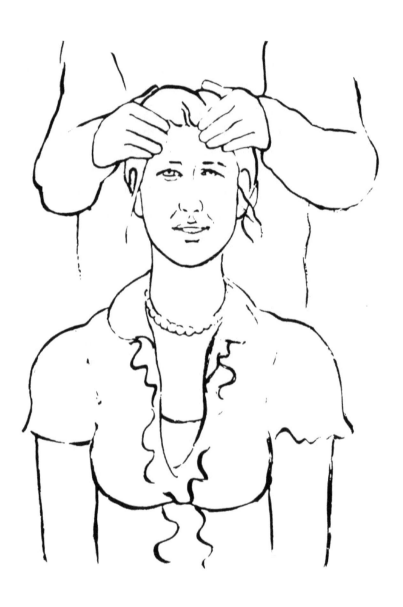

Note that animals can benefit from the 'Stress Aspirin' too.

My dogs used to be terrified during Bonfire Night. Once I found one dog staring at me, with his big eyes, from inside my bedroom cupboard and when I opened the fridge door, the other dog wanted to squeeze into it, possibly to hide, even though there was no room.

He was so strong that I could not close the door and, in desperation I held his neurovascular points and called my husband to do the same to the dog in my cupboard.

Gradually they stopped shivering with fear and as their points began to balance they calmed down and found refuge under the kitchen table where they sat quietly during the noise of the fireworks' display outside our house on the green.

After the fireworks had finished we put the dogs on a lead and encouraged them to come outside with us. We were amazed how relaxed they were, sniffing about to find bits of discarded sausages.

THE IMPORTANCE AND SIGNIFICANCE OF POSTURE

"Structure governs function. Function has an effect on structure"

This is the osteopath's motto. When there is optimal function of the muscular and skeletal system, especially the spinal column, we enjoy good health.

Good posture helps muscles to move freely and allows flexibility. When our posture is good, the bones and ligaments of the skeletal system can counteract the pull of gravity. When we shift our body weight, our muscles can adjust the centre of gravity to keep us upright. We feel alive, moving and vibrant.

Poor posture puts a strain on muscles and ligaments. This can generate pinched blood vessels, which restricts circulation and locks stiff joints. Slouching can even compress and seriously affect the functioning of our digestive and respiratory system. This can cause us to trip or fall over. When we override the integrity of muscle tone, the body sends signals to us in the form of tension or even pain.

The spine is the central part of the nervous system, maintaining a healthy posture and strong lower back. Any interference caused by poor posture can affect how we feel and communicate with other body systems. Between each vertebra of the spine are nerve reflexes passing information continually to and from the body, as well as during breathing. This process takes place even when we are asleep.

Muscles are attached to our bones by tendons. These are designed to be flexible enough to allow bones to move whilst at the same time strong enough to support the body's natural structure.

114

When the symmetry of the muscles is challenged, the balance of energy is affected and this is often the cause of painful muscles, neck, back or knee pain, shoulder tension or breathing difficulties.

If posture has been neglected, any deviations can affect the structural health and functioning of our body. Poor posture can also affect the free flow of meridians, the draining of neurolymphatic points, other bodily systems and our energy in general.

When babies start to sit up, you may have noticed their bolt upright position. As they increase their movements, the muscles begin to adjust and the spine gradually develops into a natural shape or curve.

HOW TO CHECK YOUR POSTURE

To check whether your muscles are balanced: stand in front of a mirror or a friend. Observe the following:

• Do I feel any tension or pain?

• Are my knees relaxed?

Visualise a plumb line that passes down from the head to the feet. Now follow the plumb line. Correct posture is when the line of gravity of the plumb line falls:

• Behind the ear

• Behind the shoulders

• Through the knee

• In front of the ankle bone.

When looking at your posture you might like to make a note of the following:

• Am I holding my head straight or is it tilted to one side?

• Are my shoulders level?

• Are my hands turned differently to each other?

• Are my hands and elbows held away from the body?

• Is my belly hanging forward?

• Are my knees hyper-extended (knee is pushed too far back)?

• Am I leaning forward?

• Is one of my ankles turned inwards?

• Do I have flat feet?

- Is my foot turned in?
- Is my foot turned out?
- Can I place my hands behind my back with ease?
- Can I raise my arms with ease?

LOOK AT YOUR POSTURE . . .OTHERS DO

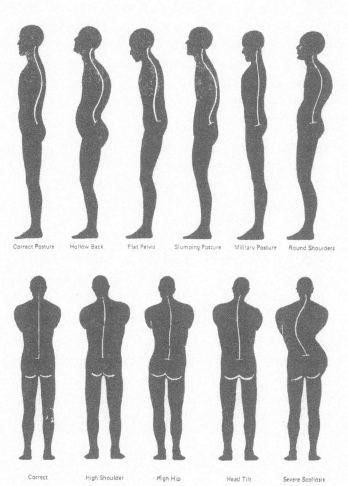

Correct Posture · Hollow Back · Flat Pelvis · Slumping Posture · Military Posture · Round Shoulders

Correct · High Shoulder · High Hip · Head Tilt · Severe Scoliosis

DAILY POSTURAL AWARENESS CHECK

When you sit down, sit right back and try and move your bottom to the furthest point away from the body until you make contact with the back of the chair.

Then create a space between the upper part of the hips and lower part of the ribcage by gently moving your upper body upwards (growing tall) without raising your shoulders. The shoulder blades should now be in contact with the back of the chair. This helps your shoulder blades to drop back and allows your head to move freely. Try this also when you sit in your car before you drive. The same applies when you are standing or walking. Ensure that your knees are supple and not pushed back.

If the above posture causes you discomfort or pain, do NOT try to enforce this procedure. You might like to seek a chiropractor or osteopath for a check-up. Or better still, try to locate an experienced Touch for Health (TfH) practitioner for a muscle balance. Your therapist can also identify whether the muscle imbalance is due to other physical health problems, nutritional imbalances or caused by emotional stress. If your problem is of a structural nature, they can refer you to an osteopath or chiropractor.

As mentioned before, we regularly service our cars, central heating and lawn mowers, but often do not consider giving 'service' to our body. Most of my patients return regularly for a six monthly body MOT in TfH and it is very gratifying for me to see when they leave refreshed.

Whenever I see a patient for the first time, I use discreet face reading and check for other symptoms that they are unaware they are displaying. I can also take note of their postural weaknesses.

The following case history is typical of how I know which treatment a patient needs as a priority.

My husband advised one of his fellow solicitors to see me about his back pain. As soon as he walked into my therapy room, I was aware that his sacrospinalis muscles needed attention. These muscles are a group of separate muscles which run along both sides of the spine. These many small muscles enable the spine to keep the back erect. Malfunction of this muscle group is often related to many health problems, such as back/shoulder/elbow pain, bladder problems or emotional strain, amongst many other symptoms.

I asked him to stand up so I could check his posture – his knees were firmly locked back. This caused the head to tilt forward and, in turn, caused extreme tension on his sacrospinalis muscles. I asked him whether he had suffered any injuries. He had none to report and he told me that he had fruitlessly visited many specialists and had undergone numerous X-rays and MRI scans to no avail.

After I administered the treatment in TfH and explained how his poor posture had affected the free flow of muscle responses to and from his spine, he told me that, as the son of an African chief, he had had to endure hours of standing as erect as possible next to his father during parades. "My back was killing me, but I didn't want to admit this to my father. I have no problems sitting, but within a few minutes of standing, I suffer extreme back pain."

Some years later when I accompanied my husband to an international law convention in Hong Kong, we met again. To my extreme embarrassment he knelt down on his knees in front of me and kissed my feet. He said, "You are my goddess of health. I have not had to suffer any more back pains since I saw you."

THE VITALITY OF WATER

"You may not be sick; you may be thirsty, or you may be dehydrated!"

Our bodies are made up of over 70% water and our brain mass of over 80%. Scientific truth and thinking is that water acts as a solvent in the body to carry nutrients to body cells and is responsible to regulate all functions in the body. In the cell membrane there is hydroelectric energy. Water helps the distribution and transportation of hormones, chemical messages and nutrients to and from organs and is important for activating and regulating neurotransmitters.

Our brain has electrolytic functions to perform and our acupuncture points are magnetic in appearance. For energy to flow freely we need water. With dehydration the level of energy and regeneration of the brain is decreased and many functions of the brain that depend on this type of energy become inefficient.

If you were challenged to write about the importance of water and its effect on your body, could you fill one page?

In his book 'Your Body's Many Cries for Water', Dr. F. Batmanghelidj studied the mental and other health problems of many patients. His 150-page report makes fascinating reading; each page is an education in itself.

During his extensive clinical and scientific studies he discovered that the damage caused by chronic dehydration can be the source of a factor in depression and may contribute to many health problems, such as viral diseases, ME (chronic fatigue symptom) and cystitis (inflammation of the bladder). It can also cause many common ailments and conditions like high blood pressure, hormonal imbalances, allergies, hiatus hernia, back pain, angina, irritability, lack of concentration, headaches and general lack of energy. The list he researched seems endless.

Our nervous system can be compared to electrical wiring in a house. If all the contacts are intact, no problem. However, if our bodies are dehydrated, the nerve-water transport cannot properly transmit messages.

It also needs to be understood that the kidneys are part of our blood filtration system. Improper functioning can result in unhealthy skin, acne, pimples, boils and headaches. Coffee, strong tea, manufactured drinks or excessive alcohol are considered food by the kidneys. They have to overwork but cannot filter toxins and poisons sufficiently. Drinks high in sodium (salt) can even be associated with weight gain.

Just visualise your body as a desert for a moment. Whenever there is a rainfall the plants start to retain whatever water has fallen on their leaves and flowers to provide a reservoir for meagre times. Your body can react in a similar way. Insufficient water intake and the body holds on to whatever small amounts it receives, often to be deposited in the thighs for safekeeping. No matter what exercise you undertake, if you are dehydrated your thighs can tell.

I regularly see patients with nagging low back pain. Unless there is a postural imbalance or a structural problem, muscle testing often confirms that the person is dehydrated, which can affect and weaken the psoas muscle that is directly related to the kidney energy. The psoas muscle is part of the hip-flexing group and supports the natural lumbar curve of the spine. Much back pain could be avoided, especially during gardening or physical exercise, if we could respect the body's need for water.

Our large intestines are designed to reabsorb water and salt. Correct salt intake is another ingredient for healthy bodily function. This prompted Dr. Batmanghelidj to write another best-seller 'Water and Salt – your Healers from Within' and in my view, his book should be in everybody's home library.

How Much Water do I Need?

It is easy to check whether you are dehydrated. Check the colour of your urine regularly; is it orange or a dark yellow? Healthy urine should be a very pale yellow.

If you think you are dehydrated over a period of time, it is helpful to begin by sipping small mouthfuls of water during the day. Avoid drinking too much water during mealtimes. This can affect the balance of digestive juices and enzymes needed for proper digestion.

Typically, in kinesiology we recommend drinking about 1/3 of an ounce for each pound of body weight. It goes without saying that a person who is ill, on medication or exercising needs to increase their water intake. By using Touch for Health muscle testing, your practitioner can perform a simple test to check whether there is adequate water in the body and whether water is distributed correctly.

It is helpful to start the day by flushing your body with a glass of water (this can be warm water if you prefer). Some nutritionists also recommend adding a squeeze of lemon juice, which is regarded to be helpful for cleansing the liver.

Obviously, if you suffer from a weak bladder you might like to reduce your water intake in the early part of the evening.

It has also been noted that the elderly, although they may feel less thirsty, will often lack adequate water.

Whilst in Colombo, I became good friends with the wife of the Australian ambassador. She had recently lost her sister who suffered from food poisoning and diarrhoea. Sadly, the cause of death was severe dehydration.

BE LIKE WATER

When the moonlight beckons the sea
And the waves move silent energy
Past rocks, wood and clay

When there is no way
When there is no light to flow
And your life energy is low
Let the wheels of water replenish your home, garden and soul
And let them make you whole

When your well is dry
And there is no want for fun or play
Let ever flowing water restore
And clean your body for evermore

Let the life source of water become your wings
To swiftly spring-clean your links
To empower your heart, spirit and soul

Since all our power lies in our body, mind and soul
So – be like water and flow

BREATHING EXERCISES

The breathing technique described in Focus Points can also be used here whenever you find it difficult to switch off.

There is another useful breathing exercise that is favoured by many yogis. This can be used at night when you are in bed. This is a way to be deeply connected with yourself, a way to get in touch with yourself and to look deep inside yourself.

Take a few gentle breaths and embrace silence. Imagine silence as a very open space, the space of contentment. When ready, anchor your thoughts on your right big toe. How does it feel? Are you aware of any sensations? Don't worry if you are not able to feel any difference. Then gently breathe in slowly through your nose with your mouth closed, while visualising energy moving up from your toe to your foot, knee, thigh and continue all the way up to your head. Swivel the energy around your head and then, as you breathe out, let go by pushing the air out firmly through your open mouth.

You can continue by working each toe separately and then move on to your other foot.

During this breathing exercise, be open to any sensations that you might experience in other parts of your body. Do you feel any discomfort, tingling or warmth? If you do, you can meet up with those areas during your next breath in and draw up and expel these energies as before.

If you are not used to breathing exercises, you might like to work on only your big toe for two or three sessions, until gradually you have established a regular breathing rhythm.

If you are not familiar with slow deep breathing, you can resume normal breathing in between exercises until you are ready to proceed.

I am surprised to find that many of my patients do not use their diaphragm fully when breathing. By looking at their posture (and looking at their aura) I can often find their health problems before they even speak.

The diaphragm is a flat sheet-like muscle situated below the lungs and above the stomach and solar plexus. It is designed to help the lungs pump during breathing and so helps remove empty stale air, stale blood and lymph, pollution, toxins and poisons. If there is not enough oxygen in the lungs it can affect and constrict the physical as well as the emotional being. A tight diaphragm can cause anxiety, tension, high blood pressure, panic attacks, headaches, postural imbalances and limited circulation. These are only a few of many health problems that can occur due to restriction of the uptake of the oxygen that is so important for a healthy heart/lung function. The immune system loses strength and overworks. By not regularly emptying stale air we can become nutritionally depleted.

To Check your Diaphragm:

First, take a short, deep breath.

You should notice how the fascia muscles of the diaphragm reach up to the top of the ribs and, as you breathe out, move towards the pelvis and the lower part of the spine. Very often, problems with the lower thoracic or lumbar vertebrae are directly involved with restriction of the diaphragm. Many of us tighten up this region to stifle or bury our emotions, which results in limiting free-flowing energy.

Also, a tight upper body, with the ribcage stuck as though in a vice whilst breathing, can impede normal blood circulation, affecting the maintenance of a healthy energy flow and vitality throughout the body. Unless our energies flow freely, earth energy from below (YIN) and energy from above (YANG) can impede our life force.

Secondly, place both your hands on the outside of your ribcage and notice whether your ribs and hands are slightly moving outwards when inhaling, and relaxing when exhaling. If there is no movement, keep practising. Try to take only a small breath in whilst allowing the ribcage to expand and a long, slow but firm breath out which should help the ribcage to relax. Too much inhaling can cause dizziness. I recommend you repeat this exercise only three times at first, always allowing a short pause for normal breathing to rest in between. In short, this is a combined effort with correct breathing and flexibility of the upper body.

To Practise Rhythmical Breathing

When you are comfortable with this exercise, start to integrate your diaphragm breathing with that of the upper body to create a free-flowing rhythm, like the gentle rise and fall of the waves of the sea.

Take a few gentle normal breaths and visualise your belly as a balloon. When you are ready, on your in-breath with your mouth closed, use as little air as possible but at first work hard on 'blowing up your balloon' (your belly), keeping the upper body, and especially the shoulders, still. Use the little in-breath you have left to allow the upper ribcage to expand outwards, again keeping the shoulders relaxed.

Hold the breath as high up as you can, then exhale through your open mouth by first 'deflating your balloon' (by pushing your belly firmly towards the back) and then follow by relaxing the upper body and the ribcage. Take a few normal slow breaths and start again. As before, try not to repeat this exercise more than three times. Always keep your facial muscles relaxed and your jaw unclenched. When you have established a steady natural rhythm you can keep this going without any effort.

Even the cranial bones and the spine are involved in minute movements when breathing during our sleep.

By practising your breathing exercises regularly you can keep your body strong. If you feel dizzy while performing these breathing exercises you have taken too much oxygen too quickly and should stop immediately. It is basically muscle work and muscle control rather than rapid intake of breath.

You will also find that this last exercise, once mastered, can help you to relax at night and help you to fall asleep. It can also be undertaken as first aid to relieve stressful situations, phobias or even panic attacks!

"Take the breath of new dawn and make it part of you. It will give you strength."

Hopi from 'Words of Peace & Wisdom' by Native America

THE LEARNING TREE

Whenever you are asked to give a talk or demonstration, the Learning Tree can help you to assess where you are at in the knowledge of your subject.

Have a look at the Learning Tree and **work your way up from the bottom**. See how far up the tree you can go. If you haven't reached the top, you need to take stock of your subject until you are satisfied that you have done the best you can.

THE LEARNING TREE

I know

I know that I know

I know what I know

I know what I don't know

I don't know what I don't know

I know that I don't know

I don't know that I don't know

Once you have reached the 'I know', there is no need to panic or get stressed. Remember there is always someone in the audience who has not reached the top of the tree. You know you are well prepared. If you feel insecure some *'aides memoires'* (such as a handheld note with key points, slides or visual aids) can help you to structure your presentation satisfactorily.

Begin your talk in a positive way, for example: "I am absolutely delighted to introduce you to...(your subject)" and mention, if appropriate, that there will be questions and answers at the end. This ensures that you don't get put off by someone in the audience interrupting you.

Sometimes I found in my teaching that, when my enthusiasm triggered excitement in my students and they started to talk amongst themselves, there was no need to shout "please be quiet". I simply turned my voice down with the immediate effect that everybody in the room became silent. You could hear a pin drop!

Enjoy sharing your knowledge!

THE HEALING TREE

I am sure it goes without saying that when we are in the company of happy and cheerful people with a positive outlook on life, we feel comfortable and uplifted. People suffering from depression and negativity can drain our energies and we feel uneasy in their presence.

We cannot always choose the people around us. This is when nature can become a useful means to top up our energy reserves.

When next you go for a walk, have a good look out for a healthy tree that attracts your attention – you may even have one in your garden!

Once you have chosen your tree, stand in front of it with the knees relaxed and place the palms of both your hands on the tree trunk.

Keep your mind still and simply concentrate on the contact you make with your hands. Visualise the strong and vibrant energy of the roots of the tree below you. The roots are connected to Mother Earth. Take some gentle breaths.

As you are breathing, visualise yourself becoming one with the tree. Then lift up this energy from below your feet as you breathe in and guide it gently upwards, through the ankles, through the knees and all the way up the back of your spine until it reaches the top of your head. Gently circulate the energy around inside your head and visualise the collection of any unwanted 'cobwebs' or dark shadows that are in the way. Then slowly exhale these through your mouth.

Repeat this a number of times.

Are you beginning to be aware of some warmth, or slight tingling sensation, or vibration in your hands?

Keep a gentle rhythm going, at the same time making sure you do not inhale too much air or you could become dizzy.

Don't worry if nothing happens at first. Keep practising and gradually you will find that you become in tune with the life energy that your tree is giving out to you.

This exercise can also be helpful in developing your sensory organs, which you can apply in hands-on healing.

Before you leave, don't forget to thank your tree!

CHOOSING YOUR HEALING TREE

1. ENJOYMENT

WALNUT

2. GIVING, GRATITUDE AND HUMILITY

SILVER BIRCH

3. CREATIVITY AND FULFILMENT

ROWAN

4. RESPONSIBILITY AND CONSIDERATION

ELM

5. CONFIDENCE AND TRUST

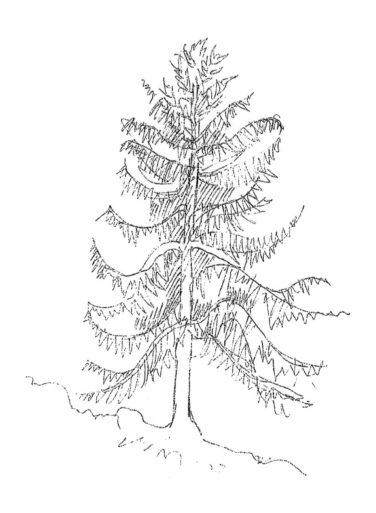

LARCH

6. DETACHMENT

SWEET CHESTNUT

7. FLEXIBILITY AND BALANCE

BEECH

8. PATIENCE

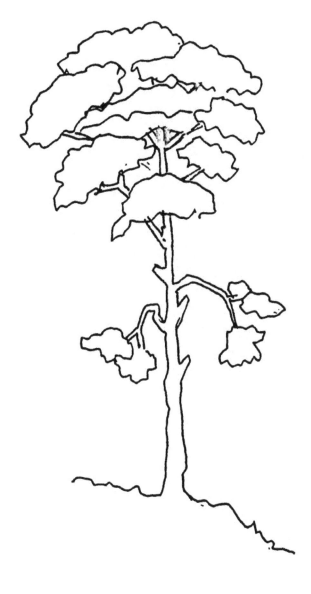

PINE

9. BEINGNESS

YEW

10. FREEDOM

OAK

EXERCISING

"Better to hunt in fields, for health unbought, than fee the doctor for a nauseous draught. The wise, for cure, on exercise depend; God never made his work for man to mend."

Henrik Ibsen (1828-1906)

If you are not used to exercise, here are a few starter suggestions:

Go for a walk

You can start by walking 15 minutes every day, rain or shine, and gradually increase it to walk briskly up to 30 minutes. After 30 minutes our body starts to burn unwanted body fats. Does this sound encouraging enough? About 3 times a week you could venture beyond the 30 minutes. Apart from stimulating your circulatory system, walking can clear your mind and can help with problem solving. Plus it's free!

Birdwatching

This can make your walk more interesting but obviously not from your living room!

Dog walking

If you don't have a dog, you could go with or on behalf of a friend.

Pilates

A series of exercises to help increase flexibility and to improve posture. This is a wonderful aid with breathing and relaxation.

T'ai chi

An energy-based exercise to empower you to help you find strength and good health. When I was in China, I was amazed to see literally hundreds of people at six o'clock in the morning who stopped on their way to work to do their exercises, whilst being totally oblivious to anyone around them.

Learning to dance

There are numerous classes on different types of dancing, such as salsa, circle dancing, ballroom dancing etc.

Racket sports

Tennis, squash or badminton are examples. You can find in every town and almost all villages groups who offer these classes. Tennis courts are also very common – most sport centres will own some.

Cycling

Get out that sad, dusty bicycle from your garage. Cycling does not impact your joints as much as jogging or running.

Swimming

The water supports your body weight and allows you to move muscles without so much pull of gravity.

Yoga

This is brilliant for both self-empowerment and relaxation – see 'Yogi Bear' on the following pages. This little bear delights the visitors at the Ahtari Zoo, Finland when he performs his daily morning exercises!

There is a whole world out there where you can find the right exercise to suit you and where you can have fun and find friendship. You will start to feel good, positive and alive.

If you are suffering from ill health, high blood pressure or are recovering from an operation, you might like to ask your doctor whether it is advisable to do certain exercises. He or she might also like to refer you to a physiotherapist as a starting point.

Anybody can do it. 'Bear' in mind to start gently

SALUTE TO THE SUN

This is an Indian Surya Namaskara exercise with roots in the yogic tradition. (Surya means 'sun', Namaskara is a greeting or salutation.) These exercises are demonstrated by 9-year-old Josh, as captured in his mother's drawings.

Josh, a very artistic child, always a daydreamer and only living in his head, found it difficult to concentrate at school. I showed him the Surya positions to help him to be more centred and calm before going to school and he took to them with great enjoyment and commitment. Whenever he remembers, he follows these exercises and at weekends gets the whole family involved.

"It makes me very happy and relaxed and I feel very calm and strong," he told me at his next visit.

The Salute to the Sun is part of a wonderful routine of exercises and worship found in the scriptures of ancient India. It is best performed at sunrise and facing East. It consists of gentle flowing movements synchronised with breath, helping to promote flexibility in the limbs and to focus the mind.

This exercise is to be performed slowly and preferably in an open space, on an empty stomach, while thinking or saying the mantras associated with each drawing.

This Surya Namaskara exercise is best to be repeated up to 3 times. To gain beneficial effects you need to continue this routine daily for at least 8 to 10 days.

A word of caution: these exercises can benefit all ages, even the elderly, as long as you work with your body's own capability of movement, and stretch while using synchronised breathing as indicated.

Take each position as comfortably as you can. In time you will surprise yourself – you might even become as flexible as our little Josh, as seen in the drawings below.

To position 1: Stand upright with both feet together and knees slightly relaxed. Then allow all tensions to go from your body. When ready, place both hands together and get your thumbs to touch your chest with your elbows pushed out. *Inhale* gently, then *exhale* and say aloud:

"I hold up my head to face the world. Before I face the world, I must be able to face myself."

To position 2: *Inhale* and raise your arms upwards and allow your body to bend backwards, follow with your head and look up.

"As I stretch I feel joyous and uplifted."

To position 3: *Exhale*, bend over and move your hands slowly down, past your knees and lower if you can.

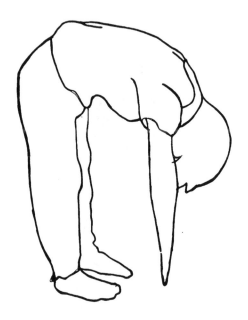

"As I bow down I am myself. I may have down moments, during which I learn to rest in my inner being."

To position 4: *Inhale* slowly whilst making a step backwards with the right leg and the toes facing forward. The hands are on either side of the left foot. Raise your hips.

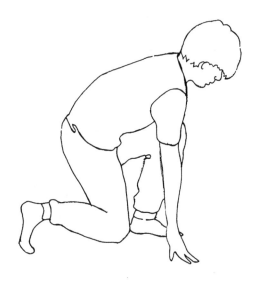

"I am ready to run life's race."

To position 5: *Exhale* and place both feet together, toes facing forward, hands are on the ground on either side of the shoulder and straight, then raise the hips.

"I close my eyes and feel the strength and balance within my being."

To position 6: *Inhale* and slowly lower the hips to the floor. *Exhale* and lower the body to the floor until the feet, knees, hands, chest and forehead are touching the ground.

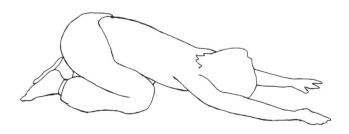

"I acknowledge the earth which is mother to us all."

To position 7: *Inhale* and slowly raise the head and bend backwards as much as comfortable. This encourages the spine to bend to the maximum.

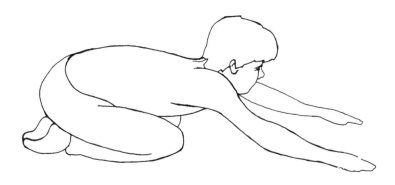

"My spirit rises from the earth in jubilation."

To position 8: *Exhale* and with the arms straight, raise the hips, so creating an upward arch with the back. Then *inhale*.

"I am as high as a mountain. I feel the serenity and strength of the mountain within me."

To position 9: *Exhale* slowly, keeping both arms straight and bend the left leg at the knee by moving it forward, making a big step, then lift the head.

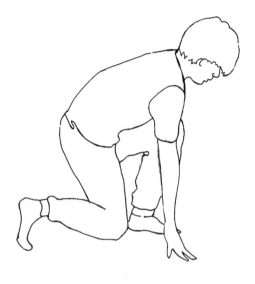

"I am filled with confidence."

To position 10: *Inhale*, and when ready *exhale*, repeating position as No. 3. Your feet and toes are now firmly placed on the ground.

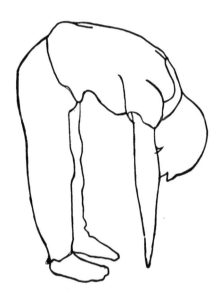

"I turn within and acknowledge my inner being."

To position 11: *Inhale,* relax and *exhale,* then repeat position as No. 2.

"I open my arms, my hands and feet to the realisation of the beauty and worth of the heavens, the stars and the sun."

To position 12: Return to the first position.

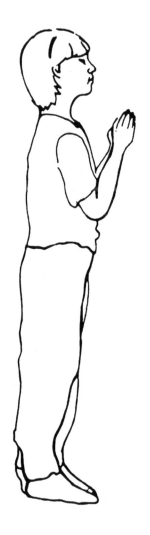

"I feel the harmony and peace within me. I am thankful and serene."

BACH FLOWER REMEDIES

Dr Edward Bach (1886-1936) trained as a doctor in London and then specialised in bacteriology in chronic disease and also in the mental outlooks of patients.

He was also knowledgeable in the discipline of homoeopathy. Homoeopathy was founded as a viable alternative to conventional medical methods by the German physician Dr Samuel Friedrich Hahnemann (1755-1843).

Dr Hahnemann used mainly natural substances: plants, animals or minerals and he observed that they have the properties of stimulating very effectively the body's curative responses.

He established the homoeopathic principle of *'like for like, the single drug, the small doses and the potentisation of remedies'*.

One of his most celebrated discoveries was when he applied his principle to the treatment of malaria by experimenting with Peruvian bark (known as quinine, cinchona or China), still used in allopathic and naturopathic treatments today.

Dr Bach was a very intuitive, sensitive man and could feel energy flows emerging from various plants. One day, he stopped at an oak tree and admired its strength. Then his thoughts reflected to a patient who had lost all courage and endurance to fight his illness.

Dr Bach was well acquainted with the homoeopathic principle 'like for like' and took some leaves from the oak tree to make a homoeopathic solution which he administered to his patient.

To his amazement, the patient began to accept his illness and started to rapidly improve.

This led Dr Bach to believe that plant life can help to create harmony and equilibrium for negative emotional imbalances. He established 38 remedies, which, to this day, have stood the test of time. They are still in use today and can be bought at most pharmacies and health food shops in most countries.

They are effective treatments for stress, severe mental tensions and negative emotional states.

Bach Rescue Remedy - Your First Aid Remedy

In addition to the 38 Bach Flower Remedies, the Bach Rescue Remedy is another flower remedy worth keeping on you at all times. Rescue Remedies consist of 5 Bach remedies: Impatiens, Star of Bethlehem, Cherry Plum, Rock Rose and Clematis. Rescue Remedies are extremely useful to have at hand as first aid and can be effectively and safely used by you or given to others for the following:

- After accidents
- Shock
- Panic attacks
- Bad news
- Sorrow at a funeral

- Before exams, driving tests or job interviews
- Stage fright.

Are Bach Remedies Safe?

Bach Remedies are natural remedies and have no side effects, nor are they habit-forming when taken sensibly. They are not intended to replace medications prescribed by your doctor, yet they can be extremely helpful when used as first aid for stress, accidents or negative mental outlook. They are generally safe to use for children, animals and pregnant mothers. However, if you are pregnant, it is best to check with your doctor.

Bach Remedies contain alcohol and so are not recommended if the recipient is an alcoholic or on alcohol withdrawal.

Dosage

From 2 to 4 drops in a little water and, depending on circumstances and age, to be taken 2 to 3 times a day. Recommended use for babies, children and nursing mothers: 1 drop in water. If the recipient is unable to swallow, you can put 1 or 2 drops straight on the lips, on the wrists or behind the ears. You can even obtain a hand-spray for ease of use.

THE BACH FLOWER REMEDIES TO USE WITH THE TEN QUALITIES

From the dictionary of the 38 Bach Flower Remedies

I have selected 14 Bach Flower Remedies to complement the Ten Qualities. They are designed to help you to create a healthy attitude and to balance negative feelings — needed to take control of your everyday life.

1. ENJOYMENT

Positive aspects	Negative emotional states
AGRIMONY trust oneself and be positive	inner mental torture whilst putting on a brave face
HONEYSUCKLE enjoy and be open to life and to new challenges	nostalgia, homesickness, one's mind lives in the past

2. GIVING, GRATITUDE AND HUMILITY

Positive aspects	Negative emotional states
CENTAURY knows when to give with humility	can't say no, loss of individuality, always ready to please
PINE responsible for the self and not blaming others when they hurt one's feelings or attention	Self-blaming and aiming to please, overworks, guilt complex, when giving always expects return and attention, interfering

3. CREATIVITY AND FULFILMENT

Positive aspects	Negative emotional states
SCLERANTHUS can go with the flow, knows own path to creativity and fulfilment	indecision, moody, lack of taking opportunities
GENTIAN knows that no obstacle is too great	easily discouraged and despondent when faced with obstacles

4. RESPONSIBILITY AND CONSIDERATION

Positive aspects	Negative emotional states
ELM does not lose hope or doubt own power when feeling overwhelmed and challenged by many responsibilities	sudden feeling of being overwhelmed and despondent by responsibilities, loss of positive awareness and lack of confidence

5. CONFIDENCE AND TRUST

Positive aspects	Negative emotional states
LARCH self-confidence and trust to success, self-assured in one's skills	lack of confidence in one's skills, fearful of failure before exams or job interviews
OAK self-decisive, reliable, stable and has positive courage to succeed under all conditions, determined and not set back by failures	brave and knows is capable yet overworks and exceeds limit of strength, can result in a nervous breakdown

6. DETACHMENT

Positive aspects	Negative emotional states
OAK self-decisive, reliable, stable and has positive courage to succeed under all conditions, determined and not set back by failures	brave and knows is capable yet overworks and exceeds limit of strength, can result in a nervous breakdown
OLIVE to live and let others live to be who they want to be, can restore peace of mind, interest, enjoyment and vitality	too tired and exhausted to enjoy that which once gave pleasure, loss of vitality after suffering under stressful conditions or illness

7. FLEXIBILITY AND BALANCE

Positive aspects	Negative emotional states
BEECH tolerance and sympathy towards others and their shortcomings, live and let live attitude	intolerance, lack of sympathy, critical towards others, hard taskmaster to the self, can cause loneliness

8. PATIENCE

Positive aspects	Negative emotional states
IMPATIENS disciplined and calm, tolerant towards others, can encourage and appreciate others, easy-going	nervous and irritable individual, cannot tolerate people who are too slow, can cause hasty actions and wrong decision-making, a loner
AGRIMONY trust oneself and be positive	inner mental torture whilst putting on a brave face

9. BEINGNESS

Positive aspects	Negative emotional states
HEATHER respect for others and the world around them, selfless, a good listener, always willing to help	too obsessed by problems, self-centred , makes too big a deal for things resulting in them being avoided, a loner

10. FREEDOM

Positive aspects	Negative emotional states
WALNUT can stand up for the self, is responsible for one's own life, being positive, content, relaxed, natural and humble, trusts the process of life	oversensitive to outside influences, lack of determination to see ideals and ambitions through, difficulty in breaking the link with forceful people, lack of self-protection during transition stages, such as puberty, menopause or even moving house

Of course, there is always the Rescue Remedy for emergencies!

CRYSTAL SELF-HEALING

Gemstones and crystals have been widely appreciated for thousands of years and used throughout history in religion and folklore be it as adornments or to enhance healing vibrations.

Archeologists have discovered a number of crystal skulls from the ruins of Mayan temples; one of these can be found in the Museum of London. The Indians of North America, the Aborigines of Australia and the ancient Chinese believed in the sacred power of crystals.

Before you start using your chosen crystal, it is important to cleanse it first and every time after its use. This is not only to clean off dust or dirt but will also clear away previous energies you attracted during its use.

There are some crystals which respond better to different methods of cleansing. However, the ones I have chosen for you to use with the Ten Qualities work well as follows: simply hold your crystal with both hands under running water. Close your eyes and visualise white light entering the crown of your head (cosmic healing energy) and guide it through your arms and hands and let the water run through the crystal.

Don't worry if you can't see the light; the intention is all that you need for the cleansing to be effective, it needs a little practice. Then finish by saying thank you.

Once you have chosen your crystal and it is well cleansed, place it into your right hand until you can feel a vibration or warmth and allow the energy to penetrate. This may take some practice. This applies also when you are choosing a crystal and you are not sure which one is best suited to you.

Then hold it directly to the area of your body, as recommended on the chart below, or simply keep holding it in your right hand. Slow down your breathing and take 3 normal relaxing breaths. Then repeat the affirmation 3 times aloud for 3 days. During the affirmation or 'mantra', always visualise your exhalation breath going towards the crystal.

A positive intent and respect when healing with crystals and saying the affirmations is needed to have an impact on their effectiveness. They can also be helpful when on prescribed medicine, by making the energy field more receptive to treatment. On many occasions, when I use bioenergy healing or am working with crystals, my patients often recall seeing, with amazement, the colour of the chakra I am working with, while their eyes are closed.

I hope you enjoy the feeling of the calm, healing vibration of crystals. Whenever I use crystals in my healing work, I call them my solid friends, a gift from our Mother Earth to be shared with all. Appreciate their strength and beauty!

Remember, should you like to wear your crystal all day, it is necessary to purify it at night to get rid of the negative vibrations it may have collected during the day. Also ensure that nobody else handles your crystal.

1. ENJOYMENT

Rose Quartz

Affinity: heart chakra

Enjoyment is a blending of all our senses and it releases the feel-good factor of endorphins which relate to the endocrine system.

The feeling of self-healing with joy affects our emotions and our mental and physical balance. All of us are individual beings and have our own perception as to what gives us joy, love, laughter, taste etc. and our five senses are instantaneous communications from outside responses.

Since rose quartz is associated with the heart chakra, it can open up awareness to the natural beauty that surrounds us and can help dissolve gloom and despondency. This crystal energy can be the bringer towards self-confidence and self-acceptance.

Rose quartz is not to be confused with our ego. It can provide unconditional love of self and towards others. By being flexible in our hearts, it brings joy into our lives.

Affirmation with Rose Quartz

"I find in every day something beautiful and new for me to appreciate, creating a positive energy to my well-being."

2. GIVING, GRATITUDE AND HUMILITY

Peridot

Affinity: heart and solar plexus chakras

It has often been said that in giving we also receive (like for like according to the cosmic law).

Peridot is in tune with earth messengers and teachers to make us aware of selflessness and humility. This crystal energy provides the combination of a golden sunrise and the clear green tone of balance, revitalising the senses of our inner light and inner strength, in short, a communicator to help quieten our inner being and to help build on our inner strength.

Once we are open to our self-awareness and self-confidence, we can become appreciative and encouraged to express the joy and optimism we have when we give or receive. Remember, your gift of self is priceless – believe in yourself!

Affirmation with Peridot

"Inner joy lights my way and I share that joy with others."

3. CREATIVITY AND FULFILMENT

Carnelian

Affinity: 2nd chakra (lower abdomen)

Creativity is a sacral energy.

Whenever we feel stuck in our way and need to move forward with vitality and direction, the crystal energy of carnelian can enable us to be able to express our self-awareness and hidden talents.

Everybody has a need to form an artistic ability, however small it may seem (e.g. writing, drawing, painting, sowing, singing, cooking, exercising). Carnelian can help you to go beyond your judgement and that of others. Whatever is pleasing to the individual's own creativity is that which brings fulfilment and this is an aspect of creativity.

There is no fixed idea as to what is pleasing to the individual and their own creativity: do not judge, just simply let it flow.

Affirmation with Carnelian

"I am open to using my many talents to express my creativity. My conscious mind is quiet and calm. I can achieve fulfilment."

4. RESPONSIBILITY AND CONSIDERATION
Lapis Lazuli
Affinity: 6th chakra

The frequency of lapis lazuli helps to ameliorate our energy system to encourage us to be more focused in our mind.

Responsibility is a state of being and not always of our own choosing. To learn to be responsible for ourselves and how we are, act or react, this crystal can help you to be more clear-sighted. Consideration is less immediate and more detached.

This is where lapis lazuli can facilitate making the right decisions, whilst still having a choice and being sympathetic in our understanding.

Affirmation with Lapis Lazuli

"I seek truth in understanding my experiences, while still having a choice."

5. CONFIDENCE AND TRUST

Ametrine

Affinity: 3rd & 6th chakra

Very often we find it difficult to show boldness and self-belief.

Ametrine can encourage you to move from negative constraints to your positive qualities. At the same time, this crystal has a dual aspect: to connect you with the deeper meaning of trust, firm belief and resilience – our inherent knowing. Ametrine is a combination of Amethyst and Citrine.

This frequency helps to synthesise and build confidence in its interaction within both of the above two chakras; a connecting passage to calming and clearing the mind, body and spirit.

Affirmation with Ametrine

"I think and communicate clearly, synthesising information from all levels of my being. With clarity I have more confidence in myself."

6. DETACHMENT
Rutilated Quartz
Affinity: all 7 chakras

If we need to be in control, to separate or find some space to disconnect, reflect and to have no reaction or any judgement, we need to learn to be detached.

Rutilated quartz is a route to your inner journey of the self and to be able to judge the right time for cutting ties, forgetting any injustices, releasing anger and forgiving yourself and others. This quartz can help you to create a spiritual union to become a better person and to replace your negativity with unconditional love.

Rutilated quartz has a deep penetrating energy and seeks areas within your inner being when you need to get to the root and core of troublesome thoughts. It helps release memories and feelings and clears old patterns that have outlived their usefulness.

Affirmation with Rutilated Quartz

"I can now see clearly beyond the past. I release all expectations. The moment is now. I am rebuilding my life. I have a new beginning."

7. FLEXIBILITY AND BALANCE

Black Tourmaline

Affinity: 1st chakra

Flexibility is a movement to be open to change by using versatility and spontaneity: a good quality to possess in today's life of continual last-minute changes.

Whenever you feel that your thinking is not flexible to change and your body becomes stiff and rigid (as we think is as we become), this crystal can become an aid to communicating readily to unforeseen circumstances, to help you to stay balanced and flexible in your well-being, what you eat, what keeps you healthy and how you think.

The dual frequency of black tourmaline helps to focus on our own flexibility and balance.

Affirmation with Black Tourmaline

"Completing one step at a time connects me with my inner roots and gives me a sense of continuity in my life. I am flexible and I am balanced."

8. PATIENCE

Blue Calcite

Affinity: 3rd and 6th chakra

We are not always endowed with patience and self-control. We want everything here and now!

Blue calcite is an aid to calming the nervous system whilst waiting for perspectives. This means to be able to communicate readily whilst staying calm without emotions or anger or response to urgency.

This crystal is helpful in promoting a more healthier, more balanced and calmer aspect as to how life can become, and helps one to not react irrationally, especially if the body wants an outlet for lack of reasoning.

Affirmation with Blue Calcite

"I reflect calm and inner peace with understanding and patience with life."

9. BEINGNESS

Amethyst

Affinity: 3rd, 7th chakra and thymus

The crystal amethyst is helpful to accept being part of all and to become at one with everything. It is helpful to impart knowledge of thought and knowing that we are in communion with the great cosmic orchestra, and to view from our higher spiritual perspective. Deep down we all have the understanding of inherent knowing, so as to let it be.

Affirmation with Amethyst

"I am in a light space of transformation. I release unnecessary thoughts in my quest for beingness."

10. FREEDOM - TO BE ME

Labradorite

Affinity: 5th, 6th and 7th chakra

Labradorite has often been referred to as the 'timeless teacher' to impart knowledge and understanding whenever we limit our freedom with our own thinking and restrictions.

Lack of confidence and living up to the expectations of others stops us from being who we really are. We become slaves to our own emotions and of those around us. At the same time, to gain freedom, it does not mean to care less about humanity and nature.

Labradorite helps us to support the revelation of our own independence and to acquire a change of the way we think.

This unfolding of liberation is needed to understand freedom to be me – to be myself. This crystal helps to energise the true understanding of our own personal manifestation and motivates our self-acceptance, self-knowledge, self-freedom and self-involvement, even in spite of ill health or physical restrictions.

Affirmation with Labradorite

"To be true to myself gives me freedom to be me – to be myself. I know that I can become a better person. I now choose to be free. I accept myself totally."

Crystal Self-healing with the Ten Qualities

Quality	Crystal	Affinity
Enjoyment	Rose quartz	4th chakra (heart)
Giving, gratitude and humility	Peridot	4th chakra (heart) 3rd chakra (solar plexus)
Creativity and fulfilment	Carnelian	2nd chakra (Lower abdomen)
Responsibility and consideration	Lapis lazuli	6th chakra (brow chakra, 3rd eye)
Confidence and trust	Ametrine	6th chakra (brow chakra, 3rd eye) 3rd chakra (solar plexus)
Detachment	Rutilated quartz	All 7 chakras
Flexibility and balance	Black tourmaline	1st chakra (Base chakra)

Quality	Crystal	Affinity
Patience	Blue calcite	6th chakra (brow chakra, 3rd eye) 3rd chakra (solar plexus)
Beingness	Amethyst	7th chakra (crown) 5th chakra (throat) 3rd chakra (solar plexus)
Freedom	Labradorite	7th chakra (crown) 6th chakra (brow chakra, 3rd eye) 5th chakra (throat)

AFTER WORDS

I hope you have found at least one or two simple gems you can use for your improved well-being in this brief guide.

If there is one gem of wisdom to take away, it is simply this: nobody else can breathe for you, eat for you, love for you or be you.

The techniques I have shared in this book are not only simple but in the most part free. Taking responsibility and control of your own health is a key decision to make in order to take control of your own life.

Apart from the obvious benefits, some other beneficial side effects come from taking such responsibility for yourself.

You become luckier in life and in love. People want to be with you and around you. Life takes on an amazing magical quality.

This state of being is a joy to experience and to see in others. Helping people achieve this state is my 'reason to be'.

There is only one you who can shout from the rooftops: "I AM FREE TO BE ME!!"

FREEDOM

RESPONSIBILITY AND
CONSIDERATION

GIVING, GRATITUDE
AND HUMILITY

PATIENCE

CONFIDENCE
AND TRUST

DETACHMENT

ENJOYMENT

CREATIVITY AND
FULFILMENT

FLEXIBILITY
AND BALANCE

BEINGNESS

THE TEN QUALITIES AT A GLANCE

NEGATIVE EMOTIONAL STATE	POSITIVE ATTITUDES
1.ENJOYMENT Closed mind Oversensitivity Self-defeatism	Protection from change or outside negativity Involvement
2. GIVING, GRATITUDE AND HUMILITY Overwork to please others Self-denial Selfishness	Humility Giving and receiving in equal measures

NEGATIVE EMOTIONAL STATE	POSITIVE ATTITUDES
3. CREATIVITY AND FULFILMENT Lack of joy Despondency Stagnation	Self-realisation Optimism Buoyancy
4. RESPONSIBILITY AND CONSIDERATION Negative outlook on life Selfish, blaming of others Defenceless	Self-assurance Accountability for one's own actions
5. CONFIDENCE AND TRUST Inadequacy Negative state of mind Insecurity	Capability Determination Self-esteem
6. DETACHMENT Inadequacy Negative state of mind Insecurity	Using one's potential Opening up to one's true calling

NEGATIVE EMOTIONAL STATE	POSITIVE ATTITUDES
7. FLEXIBILITY AND BALANCE Intolerance Criticism Egotism and conceit	Willingness to learn Respect for others Non-judgemental
8. PATIENCE Workaholic Loneliness Over-conscientious Loss of control	Calm and understanding Diligence Common sense Relaxed attitude
9. BEINGNESS Overexertion Controlling Doormat	The ability to say no Self-awareness Self-confidence
10. FREEDOM Loss of faith for the future Stagnation for new opportunities Disharmony with all and nature	Self-nurturing Subtlety Positive attitude and trust Contentment 'Onement'

SUGGESTED READING

Walther, David S., DC - Applied Kinesiology, Synopsis, SDC Systems, Colorado (1988)

Thie, John F, DC (Thie, Matthew, MEd) - Touch for Health The Complete Edition (2005)

Holdway, Ann – Kinesiology, Element Books, Ltd, Dorset (1995)

Scott, Jimmy, PhD with Kathleen Goss - Cure your own Allergies in Minutes, Health Kinesiology Publications, San Francisco (1988)

Thurnell-Read, Jane - Health Kinesiology, Life-Work Potential, Penzance

Wheeler, FJ, MRCS, LRCP - The Bach Remedies Repertory, The Daniel Co. Ltd, London

Diamond, John, MD - Your Body Doesn't Lie, first edition, Harper & Row Publishers Inc., New York (1979)

Diamond, John, MD - Life Energy, Paragon House Publishers, New York (First Edition 1985)

Roet, Brian, Dr - All in the Mind? Macdonald Optima, London (First Edition 1987)

Hay, Louise L. - You Can Heal your Life, Hay House Inc., Santa Monica, California, USA (Original Edition 1984)

Hay, Louise L. - The Power is Within You, Eden Grove Editions, London

Dennison, Gail; Dennison, Paul, PhD & Teplitz, Jerry, J.D., PhD. - Brain Gym for Business (1995)

Promislow, Sharon - Making the Brain Body Connection Kinetic Publishing Corporation, Canada (1999)

Gillett, Richard, Dr - Overcoming Depression, The British Holistic Medical Association (1987)

Batmanghelidj, F, Dr - Your Body's Many Cries for Water, Global Health Solutions Inc. (1995)

Feinstein, D.; Eden, Donna & Craig, Gary - The Healing Power of EFT and Energy Psychology, Piatkus Books Ltd, London (2006)

Hayward, Susan - A Guide for the Advanced Soul, In-Tune Books, Australia (1986)

Native Indians Words of Peace and Wisdom - Exley Publications Ltd, New York

Kahlil Gibran - The Prophet, Pan Books Ltd (1991)

Dennison, Paul, PhD; Dennison, Gail - Brain Gym, Edu-Kinesthetics Inc., California

Barnard, Julian and Martine - The Healing Herbs of Edward Bach, British Library Cataloguing in Publication Data (1988)

Vries, Jan de - Stress and Nervous Disorders, Mainstream Publishing Co. Edinburgh Ltd (1985)

Schauberger, Victor to Johann Grander - On the Track of Water's Secret, Uranus Verlagsgesellschaft mbH, Vienna (1995)

In Beauty May I Walk - Exley Publications Ltd ,UK (1997)

Chopra, Deepak, The Seven Spiritual Laws of Success, Transworld Publishers Ltd, London, (1996)

Kingston, Karen - Clear your Clutter with Feng Shui, Piatkus Publishing (2008)

Holford, Patrick - Low GL Diet - Lose Weight and Feel Great in 30 days

Alexander, Dr Fedon - The Greek Doctor's Diet

Cooper, Diane - A New Light on Angels, Findhorn Press, Scotland (2009)

Kenton, Leslie - Passage to Power, Ebury Press (1995)

Evans, Tom - Flavours of Thought, Completely Novel (2011)

USEFUL WEBSITES

Touch for Health
www.touchforhealth.co.uk

Kinesiology Federation
www.kinesiologyfederation.co.uk

Health Kinesiology
www.hk4health.com

Edu-K (Educational Kinesiology)
www.braingym.org.uk

Guild of Naturopathic Iridologists
www.gni-international.org

ACMOS
www.acmos-sbj.com/English0/method.htm

Bioenergy healing
www.zdenkodomancichealing.co.uk

Bach Remedies
www.healingherbs.co.uk

Castle Street Clinic, Guildford
www.castlestreetclinic.co.uk

The Bookwright
www.thebookwright.com

ACKNOWLEDGEMENTS

I am very grateful to all my teachers for the inspiration to guide me on my path to becoming a natural holistic practitioner. My special thanks go to my friend and teacher, the late Dr John Thie.

I would also like to give thanks to the following people:

To the late Ann Holdway, my teacher who helped me to become a proficient instructor in Touch for Health,

To Dr Jimmy Scott, founder of Health Kinesiology, through whose work and training I managed to help so many patients on their way,

To Denko Domancicz in Slovenia who introduced me to bioenergy healing,

To Dr. Naccachian in Paris with whom I studied the ACMOS Method.

To the colourful Dr. Farida Sharon, my teacher in naturopathy and iridology,

To Ann Gillanders of the British Reflexology Association, whose professional approach in teaching me reflexology gave me a good start.

Without the help and support of Lorraine Preston, my practice manager and the caring team of my receptionists, I could not have had the peace and quiet to write this book. Thank you for the smooth running of my clinic.

Thanks also to Jeanette Fleming, my very precious friend and psychic healer who helped me out in the crystal section and to Claire Hackney who provided the front cover design and artist's drawings for the book.

Eternal thanks too to Ken Bevan and Tom Evans who between them made this book actually happen.

Last but not least, I would like to thank those many thousands of patients who trusted me when I had the privilege to treat them and learn from them.

I would also like to dedicate this book to those of you who courageously seek their full potential to be 'Free to be Me'.

ABOUT THE AUTHOR

Maya Kraus is an instructor for Touch for Health (kinesiology) which she has taught to many thousands of students.

Her other qualifications are in reflexology, acupuncture, iridology, naturopathy, Chinese acupressure massage and bio-energy healing. She has appeared both on television abroad and on radio at home. She has a doctorate in complementary medicine and is a member of the Doctor/Healer Network.

On finally having reached her 'main road', she now runs the successful Castle Street Clinic in Guildford, Surrey, with her team of over twenty practitioners.

Her speciality is in dealing with anxieties, phobias and lack of self-esteem by removing old childhood patterning and achieving a positive attitude of self-empowerment. She is also experienced in working with allergies and detoxification of hidden viruses and toxins, for which she uses dowsing and health kinesiology.

She also gained a performance diploma for violin from the London College of Music.

The Journey of a Healer

On first reading you could be forgiven for thinking that this autobiography could be a work of fiction.

Maya's life story will warm your heart. It describes her amazing journey, from war-torn Eastern Europe, through the swinging sixties in London, through to becoming a sought-after healer.

She has packed into one life what many would take several to experience.

The story has a childlike quality and is a reminder that a child's eye often sees the truth obscured by the weight of adulthood.

The Journey of a Healer is available on Amazon:

ISBN 978-1-849-14276-2

You can also buy a personally signed copy by visiting Castle Street Clinic.

Castle Street Clinic

The clinic was established in 1994 by director Maya Kraus. It quickly became a centre of excellence in natural health therapies, with over 30 different therapies on offer. It is pleasantly located near the town centre and the beautiful castle grounds.

It provides help and support for particular ailments and real treats if you just want to unwind and spoil yourself like aromatherapy or reflexology.

The body's own capacity to heal itself is often underestimated. Natural health therapies aim to encourage self-healing processes, thereby allowing the body to achieve optimum good health. To take your first step on the road to well-being, drop in or get in touch.

Visit: www.castlestreetclinic.com

or call 01483 300400

CASTLE STREET CLINIC
Guildford Natural Health Centre

Lightning Source UK Ltd.
Milton Keynes UK
UKHW021523011021
391503UK00007B/175